Laughing at the King

JOHN WOLCOT ('PETER PINDAR') was born in 1738 in Devon. He was educated in Devon, Cornwall and France and he also studied medicine in London. His medical degree was gained from Aberdeen University in 1767, by external examination in Plymouth. In the same year he travelled to Jamaica and became physician to the governor, Sir William Trelawney. Upon his return to England after Trelawney's death he practised medicine in Cornwall, where he befriended the artist John Opie, who became his protégé. In 1778 Wolcot abandoned medicine and went with Opie to London, where he began his career as a satirist under the pseudonym of Peter Pindar, publishing *Lyric Odes to the Royal Academicians* (1782–5). His verses were bestsellers and he became a well-known figure in the capital's literary and political circles, greatly admired for his biting wit and social commentary. His targets included William Pitt, James Boswell, Sir Joseph Banks and the moralist Hannah More. His most important target was the King himself. In 1786 he published the first canto of his most important poem, *The Lousiad*, the five volumes of which were not completed until 1795, and in 1787 *Ode upon Ode*, which ridiculed the official yearly odes to King George III. Wolcot's verse was collected in 1812. He died in London in 1819 and was buried in the church of St Paul's, Covent Garden.

FENELLA COPPLESTONE was born and educated in Northern Ireland, reading English at Queen's University Belfast. She holds an MA in American Studies from the University of Sussex and an M.Phil in the teaching of poetry from the Universy of Exeter. Trained as an English teacher at Makerere University, Kampala, she taught English first in Uganda and thereafter in Northern Ireland, England and Scotland, ending her teaching career as acting head of a comprehensive school. She has been a publisher's reader and a reviewer of poetry, and worked on Shakespearean topics with her husband Gamini Salgado before developing her current interest in eighteen-century literature. Her home is in Rennes, Brittany.

Fyfield*Books* aim to make available some of the classics of world literature in clear, affordable formats, and to restore often neglected writers to their place in literary tradition.

Fyfield*Books* take their name from the Fyfield elm in Matthew Arnold's 'Scholar Gypsy' and 'Thyrsis'. The tree stood not far from the village where the series was originally devised in 1971.

> *Roam on! The light we sought is shining still.*
> *Dost thou ask proof? Our tree yet crowns the hill,*
> *Our Scholar travels yet the loved hill-side*

from 'Thyrsis'

PETER PINDAR

Laughing at the King
SELECTED POEMS

Edited with an introduction by
FENELLA COPPLESTONE

Ladies and Gentlemen,
Know that I scorn a prostituted pen:
No Royal Rotten wood my Verse veneers.
Oh! yield me for a moment, yield your ears.

Stubborn, and mean, and weak, nay fools indeed,
Though Kings may be, we *must* support the breed.
Yet join I issue with you: yes, 'tis granted,
That through the World such Royal folly rules,
As bids us think Thrones *advertise* for *fools*;
Yet is a King a Utensil much wanted:

A Screw, a Nail, a Bolt, to keep together
The Ship's old leaky Sides in stormy weather;
Which Screw, or Nail, or Bolt, its work performs,
Though downright ignorant of Ships and Storms.

Peter Pindar, from 'The Remonstrance', 1791

FyfieldBooks
CARCANET

First published in Great Britain in 2009 by
Carcanet Press Limited
Alliance House
Cross Street
Manchester M2 7AQ

A CIP catalogue record for this book is available from the British Library
ISBN 978 1 85754 937 9

The publisher acknowledges financial assistance from Arts Council England

Supported by
**ARTS COUNCIL
ENGLAND**

Typeset by XL Publishing Services, Tiverton
Printed and bound in England by SRP Ltd, Exeter

*This book is dedicated to the memory of
my dearest friend, Frank Copplestone*

Acknowledgements

I am grateful to Michael Schmidt of Carcanet Press for his belief that Peter Pindar should once again be brought to the reader's attention, to Judith Willson, also of Carcanet, for her patient and good-humoured advice, and to Frances Hendron of Hendron Associates, Glasgow, for all her brilliant assistance with the preparation of this book. My thanks also to Simon Blundell, Librarian of the Reform Club, for his cheerful help in the early stages of book-finding.

Contents

Introduction

This selection from Peter Pindar's twenty thousand lines of poetry presents some of his most popular poems between 1785 and 1795, a fascinating decade in the reign of George III (1760–1820). It begins with the indignant Whigs under Charles Fox mounting a campaign of ridicule against their former associate, young William Pitt, who had become the King's Prime Minister in 1784. It continues through the French Revolution and the Reign of Terror; the King's madness in 1789; the Regency Crisis which followed, and the treason trials of the 1790s when the Pitt government clamped down on British radicalism. Britain was at war yet again with France. Against the complexity of this historical background, Peter Pindar provided a vivid portrait of the controversial King, complete with all his foibles and follies, which is as much a figure of imagination as a king in an English nursery-rhyme or traditional tale.

Peter Pindar's real name was Dr John Wolcot MD. Born in Devon in 1738 and brought up in Cornwall, Wolcot did not begin his career as a satirical poet until he was forty-four. His first satire was published in 1782, just four years before the Kilmarnock edition of the poetry of Robert Burns, with whom he would collaborate in George Thomson's attempt to collect English and Scottish lyrics for ancient Scottish airs in 1793. Wordsworth began publishing in 1793. In 1798, he produced with Coleridge the *Lyrical Ballads*, with its Romantic manifesto. Byron dismissed their poetry in his satire *English Bards and Scotch Reviewers* of 1809, listing poets worth a drubbing. (He could hardly have included Peter Pindar, since his own poetry had clearly been influenced by the older satirist.) Wolcot died in 1819. Keats, many of whose great poems had already been ridiculed by William Gifford's *Quarterly Review*, wrote about Wolcot in amusement in 1820, on the death of the King. Peter Pindar outsold all the Romantic poets except Byron.

His handling of reductive 'low' satire, a tradition derived from the broad humour of the mediaeval peasant fabliaux and familiar since Chaucer's *Canterbury Tales*, derived its realistic outlook on human frailty and folly from his medical experience. No man can be much of a hero to his doctor, particularly in the eighteenth

1

century when the training of a surgeon-apothecary began with a seven-year stint as an apothecary's assistant, among whose melancholy tasks was to administer enemas to the costive in his community with the fearsome glyster-pipe. Wolcot's expertise at mixing and dispensing various kinds of rhyming verse made his adopted name famous in a very short time. Once he had negotiated an annuity from his customary publishers for the regular reprinting of his poems, it made him financially secure and, for a poet, relatively rich.

Satire was the dominant literary mode during the long reign of George III, a period of rapid economic expansion and political change, when Britain seemed almost permanently at war, mainly with France. In the burgeoning world of British art, portraiture was queen, and caricature her ugly sister, as celebrity became a cult. Dr Wolcot, like the visual caricaturists, grasped both the spirit and the commercial opportunities of the period. The creation of the character 'Peter Pindar' was one of his jokes. The 'divine Peter' was a caricature, and his speech a parody of the Theban poet who eulogised the celebrities of his day and mystified the grammar-school boys of the eighteenth century. The pleasantly alliterative name spliced together the names of the lofty Pindar and that of Wolcot's favourite childhood pet, a stubborn little donkey.

As 'Peter Pindar', this West Country doctor became the best-selling poet of his time for two main reasons: first, he made a celebrity of the King, making people laugh at their monarch's eccentricities; second, he invented a new style of poetry out of conventional models, and marketed it far and wide as quickly as possible. Like the proliferating newspapers of the day, his stream of poetic pamphlets kept up a running commentary on the people who captured the attention of the increasingly sophisticated reading public, yet his odes and epistles never descended to the level of doggerel. They remained recognisably poems, as defined by the rules of eighteenth-century prosody. The fables, tales, and songs he included among the satires made him a family favourite in an age when poetry was designed to be read aloud.

A celebrated raconteur and mimic, Dr Wolcot was an intensely convivial and clubbable man. Most of what he said and wrote was designed for the entertainment of a wide and diverse audience. Nevertheless, he was a serious poet who wrote something every day, even when he went blind in old age and could not actually see the squares of paper he was scribbling on. He was eighty-one when he died. He was buried in St Paul's Churchyard, Covent Garden, his coffin touching that of Samuel Butler, the creator of 'Sir Hudibras' whose adventures were described in a distinctively English style of burlesque satirical poetry. Wolcot thus staked his claim to a rightful place within this vernacular tradition that began with Chaucer.

John Wolcot's background in the West Country was solidly conventional and professional. One of a long line of doctors, he grew up within a resourceful, hard-working and public-spirited family that was marked by death – like King George, he lost his father when he was thirteen. Adopted by his father's bachelor brother, a surgeon-apothecary in the small seafaring town of Fowey, Wolcot was well educated in the classics at local grammar schools. Nonetheless, he resented his removal from Devon and the small free grammar school in Kingsbridge where he had been praised for his translation of classical texts into English poetry by a kindly Quaker headmaster. He disliked his strict and overbearing childless aunts who managed his uncle's apothecary shop. His family disparaged his interest in poetry, music and painting as 'a dangerous interruption to business', sowing the seeds of his defiance and resentment of authority. He became known among his school fellows for his sardonic humour and skill in sarcastic repartee. Writing admiring lyrics to young girls of the family's acquaintance and publishing them in small magazines occupied much of his free time as an adolescent, away from the pestle and mortar. The chiming sounds of the various utensils of his trade, he claimed, formed the basis of his rhythmical skill in poetry. He genuinely did not want to become a doctor and the twelve years of training for this profession were trying to a soul longing for creative outlets little admired by a community which wrestled a living from their ancient pursuit of tin mining and from the sea.

Two formative events marked that long period of preparation. One was a mysterious year in France before he began his apprenticeship at seventeen. Wolcot never discussed his reasons for going there. He returned with fluent French but a hatred of France. He despised the French, calling them 'shrugging dogs', ridiculing the peasantry's superstitions, and exempting only Voltaire and La Fontaine from his diatribes on French treachery and cold self-interest. His suspicion of France would stand him in good stead during the French Revolution. The other was his two-year stay studying anatomy and chemistry in London, from 1762 to 1764. Memorable performances in the theatre and the chance to hear good musicians captivated his imagination. Briefly free from family pressures, he perceived opportunities in that artistic world for someone of his varied talents.

In 1767, after Wolcot had obtained an external M.D. from Aberdeen University, a Cornish neighbour, Sir William Trelawney, offered him a post as his personal physician in Jamaica. A post captain brought up in the navy, and a supporter of Pitt the Elder as a Member of Parliament, Trelawney had gained the governorship of the island through the patronage of the rich and radical Earl of Shelburne. All the Governor's entourage were presented to the King and Queen at the Court of St James. In ceremonial garb, Wolcot got to meet his sovereign in the flesh. In fact, he almost fell on him. His unaccustomed sword got caught between his legs and sent him 'nosing the ground' for several yards, causing public amusement.

In Jamaica, the convivial Governor called upon his physician to act as his Master of Ceremonies. This social role, entertaining the company with his fiddle-playing, songs and poetry, gave Wolcot an audience, a sense of importance and a good deal of poise that he was hitherto conscious of lacking. Equally valuable was the opportunity to learn from Trelawney the realities of British politics and patronage. The Governor ruled Jamaica independent of party obligations, but the only advancement he could offer his friend was through the riches of the Anglican Church. Somewhat cynically, since Wolcot had no discernable Christian faith, Trelawney dispatched him to be ordained by the Bishop of London in order to take up the lucrative living of St Anne's where the incumbent was dangerously ill – a post worth £1,500 per year.

It took only a day for Wolcot to become a priest, on 25 June 1769, but he did not return to Jamaica until March 1770. A medical student in London at the height of the John Wilkes' affair, he could now read the mysterious 'Junius' letters in the *Daily Advertiser*. Gossip in the coffee-houses pointed at Trelawney's patron Shelburne. The King, resenting Shelburne's earlier support of Wilkes in the Lords, had peremptorily thrust him out of office; Shelburne had pulled the Earl of Chatham with him in his fall from short-lived royal favour. 'Junius' redefined for the English their historic constitutional rights as individuals, particularly with regard to freedom of speech and of the press, and drew attention to how the government had infringed them, upbraiding the King himself. His daring, style and wit won him a large following. Wolcot learned much from this audacious attempt to hold the unaccountable responsible for their actions.

He had delightedly resumed a somewhat bohemian social life among London's musicians, artists and writers, taking painting lessons from the celebrated landscape painter Richard Wilson. Some of his songs were set to music by Jackson of Exeter. Life seemed promising, but when he returned, the Reverend Wolcot, who had come to Jamaica solely to seek financial independence, now found that the incumbent of St Anne's had fully recovered his health. The only available parish paid half the promised sum and Wolcot soon abandoned the priesthood and returned to assisting Trelawney with his official functions. With the help of his Cornish friends, he had a slim volume of verse, *Persian Love Elegies*, printed in Kingston but, essentially, the Jamaican adventure was over. The popular Governor died in 1772. Dr Wolcot, now thirty-five, along with Lady Trelawney and the coffin of their friend, young William Boscawen, returned sadly to Cornwall. Boscawen, a son of the famous Admiral, had drowned almost as soon as they had arrived in Jamaica, Almost the only useful thing that would link Wolcot's future with this period of such mixed fortunes in the West Indies was the short elegy he had composed to mark Boscawen's death.

For the next eight years Wolcot was confronted with the daily tasks of doctoring in Cornwall, with nothing but chronic asthma and a 'mahogany complexion' to show for his labours in Jamaica. Nevertheless, another 'apprenticeship' was just beginning. John Wolcot rapidly became the satirical bane of his colleagues' lives in Truro, where he set up practice in 1773. Venality, hypocrisy and pomposity were the targets of his sarcastic verses. Apothecaries, two of them members of Truro Corporation, were a special hate. Wolcot could tell that they were not using expensive ingredients in the medicines they dispensed and charged for. Doctors who favoured excessive bleeding were another: a song called 'Truro Roast Pork' celebrated the suspiciously large pigs kept by some of them. The local MP was plagued by Wolcot's satirical sallies attacking him for ignoring his humbler relations in his relentless climb up the social ladder. Adored by the poor, whom he treated free and often fed as well, and by the well-educated, who appreciated his satires, the sardonic doctor grew unpopular enough to be threatened with prosecution. Forced to move his practice to the Falmouth area, disappointed in love, Wolcot was in the grip of a mid-life crisis. Despite the success of his often unconventional methods, he was now ready to abandon his profession.

He left Cornwall for London in 1781 in order to launch his protégé John Opie as a portrait-painter. Wolcot had discovered

Opie as an apprentice mine-carpenter in St Agnes. Taking him into his home in Truro, he had trained the talented boy using all that he knew about art. He also schooled Opie in the social skills necessary to succeed in this lucrative new profession. Local gentry assisted by commissioning portraits and, at Wolcot's request, entertaining the boy at a level that ensured he acquired sufficient polish for his new career. By the time he was twenty, Opie was an assured provincial painter, but in London the wily doctor presented him as an untaught prodigy, 'The Cornish Wonder'. Wolcot would provide the necessary introductions; Opie would paint the portraits: they would then share the profits. It was a gamble that paid off for them both.

Wolcot's friendship with Sir Joshua Reynolds, the President of the Royal Academy, helped Opie succeed, but a crucial introduction was to Frances Boscawen. Wolcot's elegy for her son William had eventually been published in the *Annual Register* of 1779, where his mother found it and sought out the doctor to hear the whole story. Now, in 1781, she was poised to help young Opie through her friend Mary Delany's close relationship with the royal family. Queen Charlotte bought one of Opie's sample paintings, and the West Country nobility followed suit. Opie became an overnight success. He quickly married, and when his wife's family objected to his business arrangement with Dr Wolcot, Opie terminated it within twelve months of their arrival in the capital. Wolcot was forced to earn a living as a writer.

His friend and fellow-Devonian Reynolds, at whose ever-expanding and hospitable dinner-table he met all sorts of celebrities, including Dr Johnson, was not a favourite of the King, who would have preferred the American Quaker Benjamin West as his Academy's first President. Peter Pindar would subtly reveal the hidden politics of the Academy, anonymously attacking the King's lack of taste under the guise of ridiculing the demerits of his favourites.

In 1782 the first of Wolcot's series of Odes, or satires, on the Royal Academy introduced London to the dry, colloquial voice of this new art critic. The Ode was in the form of an exhibition catalogue in verse, taking the reader on a tour of the Academicians' Summer Exhibition. Wolcot's mischievous creation Peter Pindar was the wry and comical narrator, skilfully identifying each painter's characteristic faults. Reynolds, though not fault-free, was 'an eagle among wrens'. All the eminent came in for some sarcastic comment, especially West, the King's self-styled history painter, who had the attentive ear of 'the Best of Kings' to thank for his success, according to Peter.

Wolcot paid for this first production himself. The poems were printed as pamphlets, in quarto on fine paper with wide borders and clear type, looking classy, authoritative, sturdy enough to be collected, and full enough of writing to be good value. All this quality cost money and he lost £40 on their production, but the Odes made the name of Peter Pindar as someone new to be reckoned with in the literary circles of London, always hungry for new talent.

Invited to write for the Whigs' *Morning Post* newspaper, Wolcot came to the attention of George Kearsley, a publisher who had been prosecuted over his publication of the satirical 'No. 45' edition of John Wilkes' *North Briton* newspaper, in which Wilkes had satirised the King's reliance on the advice of the not very bright and allegedly Jacobitical Earl of Bute. Kearsley had no fear of satirists, on whose account publishers were regularly prosecuted, and a successful working relationship ensued for both the publisher and Peter Pindar, who continued his assaults on the Academicians with Odes in 1783, 1785 and 1786. The pamphlets, which had originally cost one shilling went up to two and a half – but they also included tales, fables and songs. This creation of a mini-anthology broadened the appeal of the poet's work, demonstrating his scope and versatility.

'Peter Pindar' provided a liberating alter ego for the eccentric doctor, but he also fulfilled a specifically literary function. By adopting the name of a poet famous for writing panegyric, Wolcot could make his own burlesques of conventional genres and lampoons on the pretensions of the socially elevated, all the funnier, since they were framed in mock praise. Claiming to be the unofficial 'Laureate' of the Academy and its royal patron, Peter offered his helpful 'prescriptions' for success. Although his vocabulary was deliberately familiar, his imagery homely, and the tempo of his six-line stanzas leisurely, Wolcot's handling of neo-classical principles of art was assured and grew increasingly so as the subsequent Odes appeared. The reader was drawn into flattering collusion with this ironic, knowledgeable commentator who made the Academicians and their doings household names among people who would never see London, let alone Somerset House. The institution itself became comically domesticated within the English imagination through Peter Pindar's regular bulletins on its shaky progress.

Growing in confidence, Wolcot began to celebrate and publicise throughout the English-speaking world all that was ridiculous about eminent people whom he believed to be promoted above the level of their true ability through the patronage that bedevilled the cultural power structure. The autocratic President of the Royal Society, Sir Joseph Banks, who owed his scientific eminence solely to the influence of the King; James Boswell and Hester Piozzi, inventors of the celebrity biography, who exploited their memories of Samuel Johnson; moralising Hannah More, whose fulsome patrons were first David Garrick and, later, Bishop Porteous – all felt the lash of Peter Pindar's tongue, along with travellers who told tall tales, and many other would-be celebrities of the day. Even Dr Johnson was described as making an ocean roar to cast an acorn on the shore, and Jamie Boswell teased that he had given up his country 'to lead a bear'! Peter's favourite target, though, was the King whose patronage, the most powerful in the nation, was almost invariably bestowed upon unchallenging mediocrities.

Wolcot's satires were based on reliable information volunteered by a variety of disgruntled or mischievous people, some close to the throne, who derived much private solace and glee from Peter's subsequent tales and observations. The loyalties of the poet were patriotic rather than political. Claiming not to be the tool of party or faction, Wolcot depicted Peter as loyal to King and Country, while attacking the government. The principles that gave the satires their force were moral, without being religious or radical. The King should recognise true merit, rely on counsellors with Britain's good at heart, and share what the British people had given him as his riches with those who needed it, rather than hoarding wealth like some ordinary miser. Beneath the surface, sophisticated readers like William Beckford, whose father, as Lord Mayor of London, was the only individual to stand up to the King personally, might detect a burlesque of 'Junius', in content and style. Those deliberately slighted by the King, like Nelson, could take some pleasant revenge in laughing at the King's idiocy. Both became Wolcot's personal friends.

Why did Wolcot feel able to mount such attacks? Part of the answer lay simply in his response to the new power of the media in the period. Satire, he said, was a 'bad trade' – but it paid. Once John Wilkes had done his work of making the transactions of Parliament open to public scrutiny, well-educated journalists treated the behaviour of their rulers as falling within the public domain. Political poetry was one of their weapons. Writers lacking the connections to gain the security of a sinecure and the necessary discretion it required, turned to satire to make a living. Their skills were harnessed by the political factions at war with each other largely because of George III's desire to play such an actively disruptive role in the running of the state. There was no other way of opposing the King's will without seeking to overthrow him. Wolcot, skilled at writing different styles of rhyming poetry, was genuinely funny. He created his own following and his pen was not for hire by politicians. Offered a government pension in 1795, after his attacks on Tom Paine and the Whigs for their support of the French Revolution, Wolcot was tempted, but ultimately refused. He simply could not write in support of people who had suspended Habeas Corpus in 1794 and introduced the Seditious Meetings Act in 1795.

Reducing the power of authority figures through using his sense of the ridiculous was also part of his own psychological make-up. Almost all of his targets had hurt or offended particular friends. The King and Queen had paid Opie less than his paintings were worth, and blatantly snubbed Reynolds. By the 1780s, those who had shaped Wolcot's medical career and censured his behaviour were dead. He seemed incapable of resisting the urge to poke fun at what he could not change, even if, as in Truro, it caused rejection, beatings, duckings, nose-pullings and, on one occasion, being called out in a duel. The inspired creation of the comical, combative, quixotic 'Peter Pindar' opened the way for him to express to a wider audience all that had gone into making him the curious individual he had become. A mature professional in his forties, he was still a defiant schoolboy with a taste for outrageous jokes. Physically timid, easily cowed by stronger personalities at times, as John Wolcot, his alter ego, Peter Pindar, seemed ready to take on the world. Probably Wolcot's bravest act was to write a Swiftian satire against James Lowther, the 'Bad Earl' of Lonsdale, for trying to starve out the miners of Whitehaven. (Lowther also wrecked the Wordsworth family fortunes by refusing to pay his debts to the poet's father. A subsequent Earl remedied this as Wordsworth's patron.) Wolcot escaped prosecution very narrowly and the case was settled out of court. Gillray provided the best portrait of Wolcot (thus 'unmasking' Peter Pindar) in his depiction of the poet kneeling to 'Satan' Lonsdale.

In the main, though, the powerful ignored him. Wolcot seemed almost to have been awarded the licence to criticise freely, his capacity to entertain a means of deflecting anger and preventing retaliation. Those contemporaries who attacked him in verse found it hard to match his expertise sufficiently to get themselves into print or a decent review, until the political times changed after the French Revolution. The government then began to fund literary vehicles of their own to attack all those considered enemies of the dominant ideology. The self-styled 'Loyalist' faction set out to tar reformers, radicals and dissenters of all hues – including the free-spirited Peter Pindar – with the same brush as 'Jacobins'. All were presented as treasonable degenerates not fit to inhabit a Britain preparing itself for the Imperial dream. (This faction, and not the 'real' King, is what Richard Newton was satirising in his cartoon on our cover.)

From 1785 until 1795, Wolcot wrote his most important long poem, the mock-heroic epic, *The Lousiad*. Something like a TV comedy series starring King George III and his seemingly unending war with his cooks, it continued tranquilly on until this petty war was finally resolved, its five episodes spanning the international upheavals of ten tumultuous years. Spin-off individual sketches of the King at large among his fellow countrymen, spreading royal affability (but little of the royal cash from his counting-house) were an added bonus. This 'King' captured and reassured the national imagination, and the significance of the caricature in verse was considerable. The stories made the King's eccentricities familiar to his subjects in such a comical way that they drew the sting from his actual madness, which might otherwise have endangered the stability of the realm. In addition, Peter's ridicule deflected criticism away from the King himself and onto the poet, who came to be regarded as a blasphemous reprobate once the moral climate of the long eighteenth century began to dissolve into that of the Victorian era. The King's political mistakes were forgotten within the mythology of royal mystique in which the death of his adored daughter Amelia came to be regarded as the last undeserved blow upon the aging royal head.

This period is sometimes termed 'the age of sensibility', but more important than sensibility in the political sphere was the cult of celebrity that impinged on both Peter Pindar and the King. Until the railway speeded up and democratised travel, few people ever got to see any prominent people in the flesh, thus prints and literary anecdotes of those who led interesting or notorious lives abounded. In an epistle to a friend in 1741, the Earl of Orrery made the following observation: 'I look upon anecdotes as debts due to the public, which every man, when he has that kind of cash about him, ought to pay.' It was a debt which the prolific Peter Pindar never failed to pay on behalf of the King whose reputation among his subjects rose and fell several times during his reign. It fell when he was known to be infringing British freedoms; it rose when he was required to rally the nation against the threat of foreign invasion. All the major events in his life produced an outpouring of poetry and song: satires when he was out of favour; hymns when his health was out of danger; 'Happy and glorious/Long to reign over us'; when there was a British victory to celebrate.

With the advent of the sincerely pious George III, the King had gradually begun to be regarded as the personification of British morality, especially in times of danger. Hated as the pliant tool of his scheming mother and her supposed lover, the Scottish Earl of Bute, at the beginning of his reign, King George, genuinely pitied for his bouts of severe mental distress, ended it as a 'saint' with a 'spotless' life. Despite the fact that he was considered 'a consecrated obstruction' and, as Bagehot calls him, 'the sinister but sacred assailant of half his ministries', George, as an embodiment of the English monarchy whose personal life was irreproachable, strengthened the government, and heartened Britain, when Europe was falling apart around France. This late cult of 'the saintly King' had the force of a religion.

Those who took this particular view of the King abominated the work of Peter Pindar as verging on blasphemy. This undercurrent of disapproval grew louder in the treason-hunting days of the 1790s. After the publication of the first Canto of *The Lousiad* in 1785, the Privy Council had discussed the prosecution of 'Peter Pindar' for bringing the Crown into disrepute. The confirmation that the poem was based on fact caused that threat to go away, but later the attacks on the character of the poet grew fiercer. Peter Pindar gave his critics as good as he got. In the case of the critic William Gifford, the protégé of one of Wolcot's doctor friends, the two West Country men actually came to blows and the battle was recorded in the *Bardomachia* of their eccentric contemporary, Father Alexander Geddes. Gifford, though disabled, came off best, and Wolcot was sent home bleeding. Peter Pindar, though, reported that Gifford was actually drawing £1,000 per year from the Treasury for attacking the political opposition under the guise of literary criticism!

Gifford's drubbing was no more than Wolcot had received regularly in Truro as a physician with a sarcastic tongue. People were still talking about him, and that was what mattered to this *enfant terrible*. His own success, at an age when a lesser man might have acknowledged the defeat of his dreams, had been incredible. With a deft touch that belied the hard work that went into writing a great many poems in a short space of time, Peter Pindar won such a wide reading public that some of his pamphlets went off to their distributers at the rate of thirty thousand a day. In 1794 *Pindariana*, his own anthology, which ran to 234 pages, was printed in a run of 45,000, most of which sold. The Irish and the Americans adored Peter. Goethe translated him for the Germans.

Peter Pindar gave anything he touched a new twist, bringing to conventional forms a new audience who required an accessible narrative. His version of the mock-heroic epic in *The Lousiad* was designed to please a readership who did not necessarily know the work of Dryden and Pope – though they did know King George. The size of this host of readers was increased by the spread of daring publishers and assiduous booksellers anxious to satisfy public curiosity. Provincial papers carried expensively placed advertisements and warnings against pirated copies of pamphlets lacking the authentic engraving of the poet's face from the portrait by John Opie R.A.

How did Wolcot get away with it? One might ask the same thing about the visual caricaturists. They admired Peter Pindar. James Gillray and Thomas Rowlandson, a personal friend of Wolcot's, were both failed portrait-painters who loved his attack on the Royal Academy. Gillray originally thought Wolcot was in the pay of Shelburne, but soon began to use his poems in his own caricatures of the King. Rowlandson, who illustrated *The Lousiad*, developed his work in the better-protected territory of the erotic. Given the choice by George Canning between prosecution for blasphemy and a pension, Gillray chose the pension, and worked thereafter for the government. Richard Newton called Wolcot the 'Prince of Satyrists'. His employer was sent to Newgate Prison where Newton, a regular visitor, caught a fever that killed him before he could suffer the same fate. Wolcot would never permit Peter Pindar to meddle publicly with the King's political behaviour. He presented himself as an old-fashioned moralist, his intention in 'smiling' at the King merely an attempt to laugh him out of folly. A self-avowed Tory, he was in favour of a constitutional monarchy, though many of the long rambling poems that make him very difficult to anthologise do question its nature and continuing utility.

Essentially, Wolcot escaped because he had the tacit approval of the King's heir. The very first reader of his stories of the King was the Prince of Wales, who sent his crony, Louis Weltje, the Clerk of his Kitchens, to fetch the pamphlets early in the morning of the day of publication. Weltje was an old friend of Wolcot's, who appreciated the Clerk's superlative cooking even more than he did that of the King's cooks who entertained the poet regularly in their quarters at Windsor and Buckingham House. Wolcot's information had come directly from gossip within the Royal Household.

In 1811, as soon as the Prince became Regent, he hastily sent a page to Wolcot with a request to know how much he owed for Peter Pindar's pamphlets. The Regent could not afford to be considered a collaborator of the satirist in stories which ridiculed his father. Told that the amount was something over £40, he sent his page with a £50 note and the kindly advice to keep the change – which made John Wolcot one of the only tradesmen ever to be paid for goods requested by the future King George IV! The indignant poet responded by directing the page to pay his publisher and to take the change back to the Regent to keep for himself. The attention of a future king, not money, was what Wolcot had craved. His pride enabled him to make a widespread joke of the Regent's offer. An obscure country doctor till he was forty-four, 'Peter Pindar' had made his own way in the world without patronage, one of the first popular writers to depend solely on his pen to make his literary fortune, and perhaps the only poet.

One of the shrewdest comments on Wolcot's contribution to English literature is to be found in Benjamin Disraeli's memoir of his father Isaac, a minor literary figure and a friend of Dr Wolcot. 'They stand between the governors and the governed,' wrote Isaac D'Israeli, in an attempt to position such writers within the social scale. Peter Pindar's function was to play such a role in the culture of his times. Literary history has not been kind to him, but Wordsworth ranked him with Boileau and Pope in 1796. Robert Burns sought and received a fine copy of Peter Pindar's poetry from George Thomson as his reward for his own labours. They understood what he was about.

A Note on the Text

This selection is taken from the 1812 edition of *The Works of Peter Pindar Esq.*, a revised and corrected new edition in five volumes. It was printed in London for J. Walker, G. Wilkie and J. Robinson, G. Robinson, Paternoster-Row; and G. Goulding and Co., Soho Square. This edition was produced seven years before John Wolcot died. It sold well.

I begin with a selection from Canto I of *The Lousiad* published in 1785, three years after Wolcot began writing as Peter Pindar. The complete *Lousiad* of 2,661 lines written in heroic couplets awaits a scholarly edition. I have edited the Cantos selected for inclusion very heavily, and regretfully limited the choice to I, III, and V of the five Cantos published from 1785 to 1795, in order to offer the sequence of the narrative and enough of Wolcot's handling of the mock-heroic conventions to demonstrate his humour and his expertise as a poet working within the vernacular satirical tradition. Long digressive sections which include many contemporary comments and anecdotes, both political and social in nature, are omitted. These would require extensive notes and add nothing to the basic story of the action which is told in verse paragraphs. All omissions are shown by ellipses in square brackets. Cantos II and IV are briefly summarised.

What I have entitled 'Tales of the King' are selected from various Odes written during the ten years when Wolcot's attention was focused on George III's curious personality. He never attacked the King during his periods of madness for which, as a good doctor, he had great sympathy. After this period Wolcot's satires were directed upon the Pitt government and on the literary magazines and their writers and publishers who set out to destroy the radical movement. Although not a radical himself, Wolcot understood the grounds of their grievances and knew many of their leaders. He was, however, implacably opposed to the French Revolutionary sympathies of those Whigs and radicals who sought to influence British readers.

The anecdotes he expanded into short stories of the King's escapades among his people were embedded within long rambling poems in which he imagined himself talking to a Poet Laureate who had been appointed to celebrate the King's official triumphs, either Tom Warton or the incompetent James Pye. These stories amounted, as he said himself, to a small industry carried on by the 'firm' of 'George and Peter' in which he was 'a bad subject' to the King, and the King was 'a good subject' to him.

Notes on these texts are those of Peter Pindar himself or, if enclosed in square brackets, are my translations or comments.

Suggestions for Further Reading

Readers with access to a university library can read the full text of *The Louisiad*, annotated by Benjamin Colbert, in Volume 3 of *British Satire 1785–1840* (ed. John Strachan, Pickering and Chatham, 2003). This is a treasure house of information, though very expensive. John Wolcot's collected poetry is long out of print; as is his biography *Doctor With Two Aunts* by Tom Girtin (Hutchinson, 1959); so too are two other books, a short selection by Paul Zall (University of South Carolina Press, 1972), and a readers' guide designed for American college teachers by R.L. Vales, in the Twayne's English Authors Series (1973). However, the interested reader can access books of memoirs which Walcot's biographer drew upon, online through Google Book Search. The most important of these is Cyrus Redding's *Fifty Years' Recollections*, published in London in 1858. Wolcot had been Redding's father's doctor in Penryn, near Falmouth, and the journalist visited him often in London, when Dr Wolcot was very old but still full of amusing stories. John Taylor, another journalist, supplied many anecdotes of their long relationship in his autobiography *Records of my Life*, published in 1833. The invaluable diaries of Fanny Burney, who chronicled her life at Court during the period covered here, do not mention Peter Pindar, though she does give an even more monstrous portrait of Madame Schwellenberg, who bullied her almost to death, than the poet himself. If Wolcot's portrait of the King derives from 'below stairs' gossip, then Burney's supplies the 'upstairs' version which is almost as zany.

George the Third: A Personal History by Christopher Hibbert (Penguin Books, 1999) gives an excellent portrait of the King as an individual, and *Princesses: The Six Daughters of George III* by Flora Fraser (John Murray, 2004) provides a vivid account of the lives of the trapped princesses for whom Wolcot had real sympathy.

Kenneth Baker's entertaining *George III: A Life in Caricature* (Thames and Hudson, 2004) includes many of the most famous caricatures of the King, several with quotations from Peter Pindar's poems. *Richard Newton and English Caricature in the 1790s* by David Alexander (Whitworth Art Gallery in association with Manchester

University Press, 1998) presents a wonderful selection of the idiosyncratic, burlesque cartoons of the radical young caricaturist who died at the age of twenty-one. His cartoon 'Treason', drawn in 1798, the year of his death, adorns the cover of our book. Here Newton laughs to scorn the idea that John Bull should be considered a treasonable 'Jacobin' for irreverent treatment of an image of the King. The hearty, well-fed 'Johnny' clad in stout English working clothes is the antithesis of Gillray's savage portrayal of the skeletal French Jacobins. David Alexander, in this first extended essay on Newton, Wolcot's admirer, suggests in his Preface that 'links between visual and literary satire, and the influence of figures like "Peter Pindar" clearly need much more investigation'.

It is a pity that this pleasant reprobate had not a little more principle in his writings, for he has really a most original vein of humour – such a mixture of simplicity, archness, and power of language, with an air of Irish helplessness running through as is irresistibly amusing, and constitutes him a class by himself. His is the Fontaine of lampooners. – I know not whether anybody ever thought of turning to him for his versification; but the lovers of the English heroic would be pleased, as well as surprised, to find in his management of it a more easy and various music than in much higher poets.

Leigh Hunt, 1814

The Lousiad

An Heroi-Comic Poem

1785–1795

Prima Syracosio dignata est ludere versu
Nostra, nec erubuit sylvas habitare, Thalia.
Cùm canerem Reges et Prælia, Cynthius aurem
Vellit, et admonuit.   Virgil[1]

I, WHO so lately in my Lyric Lays
Sung '*to the praise and glory of* R.A.'s;
And sweetly tuned to Love the melting Line,
With Ovid's Art, and Sappho's Warmth divine;
Said (*nobly daring*), 'Muse, exalt thy wings,
Love and the Sons of Canvas quit for Kings.' –
Apollo, laughing at my powers of Song,
Cried, 'Peter Pindar, prithee hold thy tongue.'
But I, like Poets self-sufficient grown,
Replied, 'Apollo, prithee hold *thy* own.'

To the Reader

GENTLE READER,

IT is necessary to inform thee, that his Majesty actually discovered,
some time ago, as he sat at table, a *Louse* on his plate! The *emotion*
occasioned by the unexpected appearance of *such* a Guest, can be
better imagined than described.

An edict was, in consequence, passed for *shaving* the Cooks,
Scullions, &c. and the unfortunate Louse condemned to die.

Such is the foundation of the LOUSIAD. With what degree of merit
the Poem is executed, the *un*critical as well as critical Reader will
decide.

---

1 [Peter Pindar, who has chosen Thalia, the Muse of Comedy, as his own, begins
his comic epic with the opening lines of Virgil's Sixth Eclogue, often used to
preface a poet's work. Virgil writes that his muse does not blush to live in the
obscurity of the greenwood where his earlier verses played on simple matters.
If he should turn to things of greater public concern, to sing of battles and the
deeds of kings, Apollo, the god of poetry, would admonish him that his gift was
for simpler strains than these. Peter Pindar, lacking Virgil's modesty, suggests
ironically that his powers are sufficient to the task of dealing with George III's
'battle' with his cooks.]

The ingenious *Author*, who ought to be allowed to *know some-what* of the matter, hath been heard privately to declare, that in his opinion the *Batrachomyomachia* of Homer, the *Secchia Rapita* of Tassoni, the *Lutin* of Boileau, the *Dispensary* of Garth, and the *Rape of the Lock* of Pope, are not to be compared to it; and to exclaim at the same time, with the modest assurance of an Author:

> Cedite, scriptores Romani; cedite, Graii:
> Nil ortum in terris *Lousiadâ* melius.

Which, for the sake of the mere English Reader, is thus beautifully translated:

> Roman and Grecian Authors, great and small,
> The Author of the LOUSIAD beats you all.

from *Canto the First. September 1785*

THE LOUSE I sing, who, from some head unknown,
Yet born and educated near a Throne,
Dropp'd down (so will'd the dread decree of Fate),
With legs wide sprawling on the Monarch's plate:
Far from the raptures of a Wife's embrace;
Far from the gambols of a tender Race,
Whose little feet he taught with care to tread
Amidst the wide Dominions of the Head;
Led them to daily food with fond delight,
And taught the tiny wanderers where to bite;
To hide, to run, advance, or turn their tails,
When hostile Combs attack'd, or vengeful Nails:
Far from those pleasing scenes ordain'd to roam,
Like *wise* Ulysses, from his native home;
Yet, like that Sage though forced to roam and mourn,
Like him, – alas! not fated to return,
Who, full of rags and glory, saw his Boy[2]
And Wife[3] again, and Dog[4] that died for joy.
Down dropp'd the luckless Louse, with fear appall'd,
And wept his Wife and Children as he sprawl'd.
[…]

Now on his legs, amidst a thousand woes,
The Louse, with Judge-like gravity, arose;
He wanted not a motive to entreat him,
Beside the horror that the King might eat him.
The dread of gasping on the fatal fork,
Stuck with a piece of mutton, beef, or pork,
Or drowning 'midst the sauce in dismal dumps,
Was full enough to make him stir his stumps.
Vain hope of stealing unperceived away!
He might as well have tarried where he lay.

2 Telemachus.
3 Penelope.
4 Argus, for whose history see the Odyssey.

Seen was this Louse, as with the Royal Brood
Our hungry King amused himself with food:
Which proves (though scarce believed by one in ten),
That Kings have appetites like *common men*;
And that, like London Aldermen and Mayor,
They feed on solids less refined than *air*. –
Paint, heavenly Muse, the look, the *very* look,
That of the Sovereign's face possession took,
When first he saw the Louse, in solemn state,
Grave as a Spaniard, march across the plate.
Yet, could a Louse a British King surprise,
And like a pair of Saucers stretch his Eyes?
The *little* Tenant of a *mortal* head,
Shake the great Ruler of Three Realms with dread?
Good Lord! (as Somebody sublimely sings),
What great effects arise from *little things*!
As many a loving Swain and Nymph can tell,
Who, following Nature's law, have *loved* too well.
[…]
Not more aghast he look'd when, 'midst the course,
He tumbled, in a stag-chase, from his horse,
Where all his Nobles deem'd their Monarch dead;
But *luckily* he pitch'd upon his *head*.
[…]

What dire emotions shook the Monarch's soul!
Just like two Billiard-balls his Eyes 'gan roll,
While anger all his Royal *heart* possess'd,
That, swelling, wildly bump'd against his breast;
Bounced at his ribs with all its might so stout,
As resolutely bent on jumping out,
T'avenge, with all its powers, the dire disgrace,
And nobly spit in the offender's face. –
Thus a large Dumpling to its cell confin'd
(A very apt allusion, to my mind),
Lies snug, until the water waxeth hot,
Then bustles 'midst the tempest of the pot:
In vain; the lid keeps down the Child of Dough,
That bouncing, tumbling, sweating, rolls below.

'How, how? what, what? what's that, what's that?' he cries,
With rapid accent, and with staring eyes:

24

'Look there, look there; what's got into my house?
A Louse, God bless us! Louse, louse, louse, louse, louse.'
The Queen look'd down, and then exclaim'd, 'Good la!'
And with a smile the dappled Stranger saw.
Each Princess strain'd her lovely neck to see;
And, with another smile, exclaim'd, 'Good me!' –
'Good la! Good me! is that all you can say?'
Our gracious Monarch cries, with huge dismay:
'What! what! a silly vacant smile take place
Upon your Majesty's and Children's face,
While that vile Louse (soon, soon to be unjointed)
Affronts the presence of the Lord's Anointed!'

Dash'd, as if tax'd with Hell's most deadly sins,
The Queen and Princesses drew in their chins,
Look'd prim, and gave each exclamation o'er,
And, prudent Damsels, 'word spake never more.'
Sweet Maids, the beauteous boast of Britain's isle,
Speak, were those peerless Lips forbid to smile?
Lips that the soul of simple Nature moves,
Form'd by the bounteous hands of all the Loves;
Lips of delight, unstain'd by Satire's gall;
Lips that I never kiss'd – and never shall.

Now, to each trembling Page, a poor mute mouse,
The *pious* Monarch cried, 'Is this *your* Louse?' –
'Ah! Sire,' replied each Page with pig-like whine,
'An't please your Majesty, it is not *mine.*' –
'*Not thine?*' the hasty Monarch cried again:
'What, what? whose, whose then? who the devil's then?'

Now at this sad event the Sovereign, sore
Unhappy, could not take a mouthful more:
His wiser Queen, her gracious stomach studying,
Stuck most devoutly to the Beef and Pudding;
For Germans are a very hearty sort,
Whether begot in Hog-sties or a Court,
Who bear (which shows their hearts are not of stone)
The ills of *others* better than their *own.*

Grim terror seized the souls of all the Pages,
Of different sizes, and of different ages:

Frighten'd about their pensions or their bones,
They on each other gaped like Jacob's Sons.

Now to a Page, but *which* we can't determine,
The growling Monarch gave the plate and Vermin.
'Watch well that blackguard Animal,' he cries,
'That, soon or late, to glut my vengeance dies:
Watch, like a Cat, that vile marauding Louse,
Or George shall play the devil in the house.
Some Spirit whispers, that to Cooks I owe
The precious Visitor that crawls below;
Yes, yes, the whispering Spirit tells me true,
And soon shall vengeance all their Locks pursue.
Cooks, Scourers, Scullions too, with Tails of Pig,
Shall lose their coxcomb Curls, and wear a Wig.' –
Thus roared the King, not Hercules so big;
And all the Palace echoed, 'Wear a Wig!'

Fear, like an Ague, struck the pale-nosed Cooks,
And dash'd the beef and mutton from their looks;
Whilst from each cheek the rose withdrew its red,
And Pity blubber'd o'er each menaced Head.
But, lo, the great Cook-Major[5] comes! his Eyes
Fierce as the reddening Flame that *roasts* and *fries*;
His Cheeks like Bladders, with high passion glowing,
Or like a fat Dutch Trumpeter's when blowing:
A neat white apron his huge corpse embraced,
Tied by two comely strings about his waist;
An apron that he purchased with his riches,
To guard from hostile grease his velvet breeches;
An apron that, in Monmouth-street high-hung,
Oft to the winds with sweet deportment swung.

'Ye Sons of Dripping, on your Major look,'
In sounds of deep-toned thunder cried the Cook:
'By this white apron, that no more can hope
To join the piece in Mister Inkle's shop,[6]
That oft has held the best of Palace-meat,
And from this forehead wiped the briny sweat;

5   Dixon.
6   [A well-known second-hand shop.]

26

I swear this Head disdains to lose its Locks;
And those that do not, tell them they are *blocks*.
Whose Head, my Cooks, such vile disgrace endures?
Will it be yours, or yours, or yours, or yours?
Ten thousand Crawlers in that Head be hatch'd,
For ever itching, but be never scratch'd!
Then may the charming perquisite of grease
The mammon of your pocket ne'er increase;
Grease, that so frequently hath brought you coin,
From veal, pork, mutton, and the great Sir Loin.
O Brothers of the Spit, be firm as rocks:
Lo! to no King on earth I yield these Locks.
Few are my Hairs behind, by age endear'd;
But, few or many, they shall not be shear'd.

'Sooner shall Madame Schwellenberg,[7] the jade,
Yield up her favourite perquisites of trade;
Give up her Majesty's old cloaks and gowns,
Caps, petticoats, and aprons, without frowns
She who for ever studies mischief; she
Who soon will be as busy as a Bee,
To get the liberty of Locks enslaved,
And every harmless Cook and Scullion shaved.
She, if by chance a *British* Servant Maid,
By some insinuating tongue betray'd,
Induced the fair *forbidden fruit* to taste,
Grows, luckless, somewhat bigger in the waist;
Rants, storms, swears, turns the Penitent to door,
Graced with the pretty names of Bitch and Whore,
To range a Prostitute upon the town,
Or, if the weeping Wretch think better, drown:–
But, if a *German* Spider-brusher fails,
Whose nose grows sharper, and whose shape tells tales;
Hush'd is th' affair; the Queen and she, good Dame,
Both club their wits to hide the growing shame;
To wed her, get some fool, I mean some *wise* man;
Then dub the prudent Cuckold an Exciseman.
She who hath got more insolence and pride,
God mend her heart! than half the world beside:

7   Mistress of the Robes to her Majesty.

She who, of guttling fond, stuffs down more meat,
Heaven help her stomach! than ten men can eat;
Ten men? aye, more than ten, the hungry Hag;
Why, zounds, the woman's Stomach's like a Bag:
She who will swell the uproar of the house,
And tell the King damned lies about the Louse;
When probably that Louse (a vile old trull!)
Was born and nourish'd in her own grey scull.

'Sooner the room shall Buxom Nanny[8] quit,
Where oft she charms her Master with her wit;
Tells tales of every body, every thing,
From honest Courtiers to the Thieves who swing;
Waits on her Sovereign while he reads dispatches,
And wisely *winds up* State-affairs or Watches.

'Sooner the Prince (may Heaven his income mend!)
Shall quit his bottle, mistress, or his friend;
Laugh at the drop on Misery's languid eye,
And hear her sinking voice without a sigh;
Break for the wealth of Realms his sacred word,
And let the World write *Coward* on his sword.
Sooner shall Ham from Fowl and Turkey part,
And Stuffing leave a Calf's or Bullock's Heart:
Sooner shall Toasted Cheese take leave of Mustard,
And from the Codlin Tart be torn the Custard:
Sooner these hands the glorious Haunch shall spoil,
And all our Melted Butter turn to Oil.
Sooner our pious King, with pious face,
Sit down to dinner without saying grace;
And every night salvation-prayers put forth
For Portland, Fox, Burke, Sheridan, and North,
Sooner shall fashion order frogs and snails,
And dishclouts stick eternal to our tails. –
Let George view Ministers with surly looks,
Abuse 'em, kick 'em; but revere his Cooks.'

'What! lose our Locks?' replied the Roasting Crew,
'To Barbers yield 'em? Damme if we do.

8   A female Servant of the Palace, who constantly attends the King when he reads
dispatches.

Be shaved like foreign Dogs one daily meets
Naked, and blue, and shivering, in the streets;
And from the Palace be ashamed to range,
For fear the World should think we had the mange;
By taunting boys made weary of our lives,
Broad-grinning whores and ridiculing wives?'

'Rouse, Opposition!' roar'd a tipsy Cook,
With hands akimbo, and bubonic look:
''Tis *she* alone our noble Curls can keep;
Without her, Ministers would fall asleep:
'Tis *she* who makes great men, our Foxes, Pitts,
And sharpens, Whetstone like, the Nation's Wits;
Knocks off your knaves and fools, however great,
And, Broom-like, sweeps the cobwebs of the State:
In casks like Sulphur that expels bad air,
And makes, like Thunder-claps, foul weather fair;
Acts like a Gun, that, fired at gather'd soot,
Preserves the chimney, and the house to boot;
Or, like a School-boy's Whip, that keeps up tops,
The sinking Realm by flagellation props.
Our Monarch must not be indulged too far;
Besides, I love a little bit of war.
Whether to crop our Curls he boasts a right,
Or not, I do not care the Louse's bite;
But then, no force-work. No; no force, by Heaven:
Cooks, Yeomen, Scourers, we will not be driven.
Try but to force a Pig against his will,
Behold, the sturdy *gentleman* stands still;
Or perhaps, his power to let the driver know,
Gallops the very road he should not go.
No force for me. The French, the fawning dogs,
E'en let *them* lose their freedom, and eat Frogs:
Damme, I hate each pale *soup-maigre* thief;
Give me my darling Liberty and Beef.'

He spoke; and from his jaws a lump he slid,
And, swearing, manful flung to earth his *quid*.[9]
Then swelling Pride forbade his tongue to rest,
While wild emotions labour'd in his breast:

9   [A lump of chewing tobacco.]

Now sounds confused his anger made him mutter,
And, when he thought on shaving, curses sputter.
Such is the sound (the simile's not weak),
Form'd by what mortals Bubble call and Squeak,[10]
When 'midst the frying-pan, in accents savage,
The Beef so surly quarrels with the Cabbage.

'Be shaved!' a Scullion loud began to bellow,
Loud as a Parish-bull, or poor Othello
Placed by that rogue Iago upon thorns,
With all the horrors of a pair of Horns.
[...]

'Be shaved like Pigs!' rejoin'd the Scullion's Mate,
His dishclout shaking, and his pot-crown'd pate:
'What Barber dares it? – Let him watch his nose,
And, curse me, dread the rage of these ten toes.'
So saying, with an oath to raise one's hair,
He kick'd with threatening foot the yielding air.
[...]

'Be shaved!' an understrapper Turnbroche cried,
In all the foaming energy of pride:
'Zounds, let us take his Majesty in hand;
The King shall find he lives at *our* command.
Yes; let him know, with all his wondrous State,
His teeth and stomach on *our* wills shall wait:
We rule the platters, *we* command the spit,
And George shall have his mess when *we* think fit;
Stay till *ourselves* shall condescend to eat,
And then, if *we* think proper, have his Meat.'
[...]

'Heavens!' cried a Yeoman, with much learning graced,
In books, as well as meat, a man of *taste*,
Who read with vast applause the daily news,
And kept a close acquaintance with the Muse;

---

10 The modest Author of the *Lousiad* must do himself the justice to declare here,
that his simile of the Bubble and Squeak is vastly more natural and more sublime
than Homer's Black–pudding on a Gridiron, illustrating the motions and
emotions of his hero Ulysses. [See the *Odyssey*.]

Conundrum, rebus, made; acrostic, riddle;
And sung his dying sonnets to the fiddle,
When Love, with cruel dart, the murdering thief!
His Heart had spitted, like a Piece of Beef:
'Are these,' he said, 'of Kings the whims and jokes?
Then Kings can be as *mad* as common folks.
Dame Nature, when a Prince's *head* she makes,
No more concern about the inside takes,
Than of the inside of a bug's or bat's,
A flea's, a grasshopper's, a cur's, a cat's:
As careless as the Artist, trunks designing,
About the trifling circumstance of *lining*;
Whether of Cumberland he use the plays,
Miss Burney's novels, or Miss Seward's lays;
Or Sacred Dramas of Miss Hannah More,
Where all the Nine with little Moses snore.
[...]
Whether he doom the Royal Speech to cling,
Or those of Lords and Commons to the King;
Where *one* begs Money, and the *others* grant
So easy, freely, friendly, complaisant,
As if the Cash were really all *their own*,
To purchase knick-knacks that disgrace a Throne.[11] –
Ah me! did people know what trifling things
Compose those Idols of the Earth, called Kings;
Those counterparts of that *important Fellow*,
The children's wonder, Signor Punchinello;
Who struts upon the Stage his hour away;
His outside, gold; his inside, rags and hay;
No more as God's Viceregents would they shine,
Nor make the World cut throats for Right Divine.

'Those Lords of Earth, at Dinner, we have seen
Sunk, by the merest trifles, with the spleen:
Oft for an ill-dress'd Egg have heard them groan,
And seen them quarrel for a Mutton-bone;

11 The Civil List, we are inclined to think, feels deficiencies from Toys. For an
instance we will appeal to Mr Cumming's non-descript of a Time-piece at the
Queen's House, which cost nearly two thousand pounds. The same artist is also
allowed two hundred pounds per annum to keep the Bauble in repair.

At Salt, or Vinegar, with passion fume,
And kick Dogs, Chairs, and Pages, round the room.[12]
Alas! how often have we heard them grunt,
Whene'er the rushing Rain hath spoil'd a Hunt!
Their sanguine wishes cross'd, their spirits clogg'd,
Mere riding Dishclouts homeward they have jogg'd;
Poor imps, the sport (with all their pride and power)
Of Nature's diuretic stream, a Shower!
This *we*, the Actors in the farce, perceive;
But *this* the *distant* World will ne'er believe,
Who fancy Kings to all the Virtues born,
Ne'er by the vulgar storms of Passion torn;
But blest with Souls so calm, like Summer Seas,
That smile to Heaven, unruffled by a breeze:
Who think that Kings, on Wisdom always fed,
Speak sentences like Bacon's Brazen Head;
Hear from their lips the vilest nonsense fall,
Yet think some heavenly Spirit dictates all;
Conceive their bodies of celestial clay,
And, though all ailment, sacred from decay;
To nods and smiles their gaping homage bring,
And thank their God their eyes have seen a King.
Lord! in the Circle when our Royal Master
Pours out his Words as fast as Hail, or faster,
To country Squires, and Wives of country Squires;
Like stuck Pigs staring, how each Oaf *admires*!
Lo! every Syllable becomes a Gem:
And if, by chance, the Monarch cough, or hem,
Seized with the symptoms of a deep surprise,
Their joints with reverence tremble, and their eyes
Roll wonder first; then, shrinking back with fear,
Would hide behind the brains, were any there.
How taken is this idle World by show!
Birth, Riches, are the Baals to whom we bow;
Preferring, with a Soul as black as Soot,
A Rogue on horseback to a Saint on foot.

12 This is partly a picture of the last Reign as well as the present. The passions of
George the Second were of the most impetuous kind: his hat, and his favourite
minister Sir Robert Walpole, were too frequently the footballs of his ill humour;
nay, poor Queen Caroline came in for a share of his *foot benevolence*. But he was
a Prince of virtues: *'ubi plura nitent, non ego paucis offendar maculis.'* [Horace:
'Where so many things shine, I do not take offence at a few spots.]

See France, see Portugal, Sicilia, Spain,
And mark the desert of each Despot's brain;
Whose tongues should never treat with taunts a fool;
Who prove that nothing is too mean to *rule*.
What could the Prince, high towering like a Steeple,
Without the Majesty of *us* the People?
Go, like the King of Babylon,[13] to grass;
Or wander, like a Beggar with a pass.
However *modern* Kings may Cooks despise,
Warriors and Kings were Cooks, or History lies:
Patroclus broil'd Beef-steaks to quell his hunger;
The mighty Agamemnon potted Conger;
And Charles of Sweden, 'midst his guns and drums,
Spread his own Bread and Butter with his thumbs. –
Be shaved! No: sooner pillories, jails, the stocks,
Shall pinch this corpse, than Barbers snatch my Locks.'

'Well hast thou said,' a Scourer bold rejoin'd:
'Damme, I love the man who speaks his mind.'
Then in his arms the Orator he took,
And swore he was an Angel of a Cook.
Awhile he held him with a Cornish hug;
Then seized, with glorious grasp, a pewter mug,
Whose ample womb nor Cyder held nor Ale,
But Nectar fit for Jove, and brewed by Thrale.
'A health to Cooks!' he cried, and waved the pot;
'And he who sighs for titles, is a sot.
Let Dukes and Lords the World in wealth surpass;
Yet many a Lion's skin conceals an Ass.
Lo! this is one among my Golden Rules,
To think the *greatest men* the *greatest fools*:
The *great* are judges of an Opera-song,
And fly a Briton's for a Eunuch's tongue;
Thus idly squandering for a squawl their riches,
To faint with rapture at those Cats in Breeches.
Accept this truth from me, my Lads: the man
Who first found out a Spit or Frying-pan,
Did ten times more towards the Public Good,
Than all the tawdry Titles since the Flood:

13 Nebuchadnezzar.

Titles, that Kings may grant to Asses, Mules;
The scorn of Sages, and the boast of Fools.'

He ended. All the Cooks exclaim'd, 'Divine!'
Then whisper'd one another, 'twas 'damned fine.'
Thus spoke the Scourer like a man inspired,
Whose Speech the Heroes of the Kitchen fired:
Grooms, Master-scourers, Scullions, Scullions' Mates,
With all the Overseers of Knives and Plates,
Felt their brave Souls like frisky Cyder work,
Whizzing in opposition to the Cork;
Earth's Potentates appear'd ignoble things,
And Cooks of greater consequence than Kings.
Such is the power of words, where truth unites;
And such the rage that injured worth excites!
The Scourer's Speech indeed, with reason blest,
Inflamed with godlike ardour all the rest.
Thus if a Barn Heaven's vengeful Lightning draw,
The flame ethereal darts among the straw;
Doors, Rafters, Beams, Owls, Weasels, Mice, and Rats,
And (if unfortunately mousing) Cats;
All feel the fierce devouring Fire in turn,
And, mingling in one Conflagration, burn.

'Sons of the Spit,' the Major cried again,
'Your noble Speeches prove you blest with brain;
Brain, that Dame Nature gives *not every* head,
But fills the vast vacuity with Lead.
Yet ere for Opposition we prepare,
And fight the *glorious cause* of Heads of Hair,
Methinks 'twould be but decent to petition,
And tell the King with firmness our condition.
Soon as our sad Complaint he hears us utter,
His gracious Heart may melt away like Butter;
Fair Mercy shine amidst our gloomy house,
And anger'd Majesty forget the Louse.'

ADVERTISEMENT: As many people persist in their incredulity with respect to the attack made by the Barbers on the Heads of the harmless Cooks, I shall exhibit a list of the unhappy Sufferers: it is the Palace List, and therefore as authentic as the Gazette:–

A TRUE LIST OF THE SHAVED AT BUCKINGHAM HOUSE

Two Master Cooks.	Two Soil-Carriers.
Three Yeomen ditto.	Two Door-Keepers.
Four Grooms.	Eight Boys
Three Children.	Five Pastry People.
Two Master Scourers.	Eight Silver Scullery,
Six Underscourers.	for laughing at the
Six Turnbroches.	Cooks.

In all, Fifty-One.

A young Man, named John Bear, would not submit, and lost his place.

(Canto II. 1787)

Canto I of *The Lousiad*, published in 1785, was a great success and John Wolcot took up the story again in 1787. In Canto II he continues to demonstrate his ability to manipulate the conventions of the mock-heroic tradition in his satire on the pettiness of the closed world of the royal household, where a character like Madame Schwellenberg can dominate the King's palace and where the King devotes his attention to trivial matters as though they were on the same level of importance as affairs of state. Peter pretends to have forgotten the convention of the long invocation to the Muses in his first Canto and begins Canto II with a long digressive passage accusing them of inspiring mediocrities to become writers – among them, 'Girls in bibs' who think they are novelists, in order to escape the important task of learning to make puddings. Madame Schwellenberg's personal history and baneful influence on the King are treated as though she were some towering character in a Greek epic, to be feared as an enemy by the Cooks who take on the role of the 'Opposition'. As Englishmen they are accustomed to liberty and they appeal to English justice, reminding the King that it is the English he rules over. Thus they get up a bold but respectful petition, asking him to reconsider his rash act in blaming them for the Louse. The servants threaten him with a revolt supported by all the English servants who have served him so well for so long. All these are named and linked to their individual official tasks in the smooth running of the household. The 774 lines of the Canto conclude:

> Lo! on th'event the World impatient looks,
> And thinks the joke is carried much too far:
> Then pray, Sir, listen to your faithful Cooks,
> Nor in the Palace breed a Civil War:
> Loud roars our Band; and, obstinate as Pigs,
> Cry, 'Locks and Liberty, and damn the Wigs!'

Peter Pindar thus has much fun playing on the old cry of 'Wilkes and Liberty' as well as playfully damning the Whigs.

from *Canto the Third. April 1791*

Magnum iter ascendo, sed dat mihi gloria vires / Non juvat ex facili lecta corona jugo. PROPERTIUS. '*Bold* is th'ascent, but *Glory* nerves my powers / I like to pick on *precipices* flowers.' Peter Pindar.

NIGHT, like a Widow, in her Weeds of woe,
Had gravely walked for hours our World below:
Hobgoblins, Spectres, in her train, and Cats;
Owls round her hooting, mixed with shrieking Bats,
Like wanton Cupids in th' Idalian grove,[14]
That flickering sport around the Queen of Love.
Now, like our Quality, who darkling rise,
Each Star had oped its fashionable eyes;
Too proud to make appearance, too well-bred,
Till Sol, the *vulgar wretch*, had gone to bed.

His wisdom dead to sublunary things,
In leaden slumber snored the *best* of Kings;
In slumber lifeless, with *seraphic* mien,
Close at his back too snored his *gentle* Queen:
Unlike the Pair of modern days; that weds,
And in *one* fortnight bawls for different beds.

Blest imp, now Morpheus o'er each Princess stole,
And closed those radiant eyes that vainly roll:
Eyes, Love's bright Stars, but doomed *in vain* to shine;
For, ah! what Youth shall say, 'Those Orbs are mine?'
Then what are Eyes, alas! the *brightest* eyes,
Forbid to languish on a Lover's sighs?
The pouting Lip, the soft luxuriant Breast,
If coldly fated *never* to be press'd?
Ah! vainly *those* like dew-clad Cherries glow:
And *this* as vainly vies with Alpine Snow.
The Breath that gives of Araby the gales,
The Voice that sounds enchantment, what avails?

14 [The grove of Venus.]

The Juno Form, the purple Bloom of May,
Gifts of the Graces – *all* are thrown away.

But possibly some German Duke may move,
And make a *tendre*[15] of his heavy love;
His wide Dominions, miles perhaps nine or ten;
His Myrmidonian[16] Phalanx, fifty men.
But, lo! his *heart*, the fount whence Honour springs,
Swell'd with the richest blood of ancient Kings.
He comes not for high birth, his own before;
Great Duke, he comes to woo our golden ore,
And add (how truly happy Britain's fate!)
Another Leech to suck the sanguine State;
To join (composing what a goodly row!)
The place-broker old Schwellenberg *and Co.*
[…]
Now Silence in the Country stalk'd the dews,
As if she wore a Flannel pair of Shoes;
Lone listening, as the Poets well remark,
To falling Mill-streams, and the Mastiff's bark;
To loves of wide-mouthed Cats, most mournful tales;
To hoot of Owls amid the dusky vales,
To hum of Beetles, and the Bull-frog's snore,
The Spectre's shriek, and Ocean's drowsy roar. –
Lull'd was each street of London to repose,
Save where it echoed to a Watchman's nose;
Or where a Watchman, with ear-piercing Rattle,
Roused his brave Brothers from each box to battle;
To fall upon the Cynthias of the night,
Sweet Nymphs whose sole Profession is Delight.
Thus the gaunt Wolves the tender Lambs pursue,
And Hawks in blood of Doves their beaks imbrue:
Thus on the Flies of evening rush the Bats,
And Mastiffs sally on the amorous Cats.

Still was the Palace, save where now and then
The tell-tale feet of love-designing men,
Night-wandering Lords, soft patting on the floor,
Of Maids of Honour sought the chamber-door;

15 [An offer.]
16 [Ruffian-like followers.]

Obliging door, that, opening to the tap,
Admitted Lords to take a *social nap*,
And chase *most kindly* from each timid Maid
The Ghosts that *frightful* haunt the midnight shade:
For *very horrid* 'tis, we all must own,
For poor defenceless Nymphs to lie alone;
Since nights are often doleful, dark, and drear,
And raise in gentle breasts a world of *fear*.
Nay, were not Lords *ordained* for Ladies' charms;
To guard from perils dire, and dread alarms?
Yes; and like lock'd-up Gems those Charms to keep,
Amidst the spectred solitude of sleep.
How wicked then to fly in Nature's face,
And deal damnation on a *kind* embrace! –
Pardon, ye grave Divines, this doctrine strange,
Who think my Morals may have caught the Mange.

Still was the Palace, save where some poor Fly,
With thirst just ready to drop down and die,
Buzz'd faint petitions to his Maker's ear,
To show him one small drop of dead Small-beer;
Save where the Cat, for Mice so hungry watching,
Swore the lean animals were scarce worth catching;
Save where the Dog so gaunt, in grumbling tone,
By dreams deluded, mouthed a Mutton-bone;
Save where, with throats to sounds of horror strain'd,
Crickets of Coughs and Rheumatisms complain'd,
Lamenting sore, 'amid a Royal hold,
How hard that Crickets should be kill'd by *cold!*'

Now Fame to Discord's dreary Mansion flew,
To tell the Beldam *more* than *all* she knew,
Who, at the Devil's table, for her work,
For ever welcome finds a knife and fork:
Discord, a sleepless hag who never dies,
With Snipe-like nose, and Ferret-glowing eyes,
Lean sallow cheeks, long chin with beard supplied,
Poor crackling joints, and wither'd parchment hide,
As if old Drums, worn out with martial din,
Had clubb'd their yellow Heads to form her Skin;
Discord, who, pleased a universe to sway,
Is never half so blest as in a fray;
[…]

The form of Madame Schwellenberg she took,
Her broken English, garb, and Sin-like look;
Then sought the Palace and the Royal ear,
And whisper'd thus: 'Mine God, Ser, nebber fear.
Oh, please your Majesty, you ver ver right:
Shave all de rascal, if but out of spite.
Lord! Lord! how vill a mighty Monarch look,
Not able, O mine God, for shave a Cook?
Dat like a King, I say, what can't do dat?
Mine God! pray haf more spirit dan a Cat.
Ser, in mine Court de Prince be great as King:
He scorn to ax one word about a ting.
Mine God! de Cook muss nebber dare make groan;
Nor dare to tell a Prince, der soul der own:
'Tis de dam Englis only dat can say,
"Boh! fig for King! by God, I'll haf my way."

'I haf see Court enough, a Prince and Dook,
But nebber wish on sush as dis to look.
I say ver often to myself: "Goode God!
I nebber vish a Crown mine head for load.
I do not vish myself more greater efils:
A King of Englis be a King of Defils."
To punishment de lousy rascal bring,
And show dem all vat 'tis for be a King.
America haf cover us vid shame;
Jack Wilkes too be a dam, dam uglish name;
And sal de paltry Cook be conqueror too?
No, God forbid! as dat vill nebber do.
De Hair muss fall before your Royal eye:
'Tis someting, fegs! to triumph 'pon poor Fly.'

Pleased with her voice, the King of Nations smil'd,
For Power with Monarchs is a favourite child.
'What! what! not shave 'em, shave 'em, shave 'em, shave 'em?
Not all the World, not all the World, shall save 'em.
I'll shear 'em, shear 'em, as I shear my Sheep.' –
Thus spoke the mighty Monarch in his sleep:
Which proves that Kings in *sleep* a Speech may make,
Equal to what they utter broad awake.

Charm'd with the mischief, full on Fancy's view,
Quick to the Major's room the Fury flew;
Put off the form of Schwellenberg, and took
Of Madame Haggerdorn the *milder* look:
A woman in whose soul no guile is seen,
The Mistress of the Robes to our good Queen;
A Queen who really has not got her peer;
A Queen to this our Kingdom wondrous *dear*;
Which shows, however folks are apt to sport,
That *all* the Virtues may be found at Court.
Now in the Major's ear the Beldam said:
'Yan Dixon, Yan, you must not, man, be fraid.
I like mush your Peteeshon to de King:
Though George will swear 'tis dam, dam saucy ting;
And swear, dat, as his soul is to be save,
Dat ebbry von of you sal all be shave.
Yan Dixon, rader your dear Life lay down,
Dan be de Laugh (mine Gote!) of all de Town.
De ver, ver littel Boy and Girl you meet,
Vill point and laugh and hoot you trow de street.
De same (mine Gote!) vill Chimney-sweep behave,
And cry, "Dere go de Blockhead dat vas shave:"
"Dere go von poor shave fellow!" cry de Trull,
"Because he had de Louse upon his scull."
I know he say, dat you sal lose your Lock,
Before to-morrow mornin twalfe o'clock.
I tink dere may be battel: nebber mind;
I hope dat Godamighty will be kind.
What if de King make noise about de house,
For noting but his dam confounded Louse?
He be but *von*, you know; an den for you,
Mine Gote! Yan Dixon, you is *fifty-two*:
Tink, Yan, how George vas frighten by de Mob,
When Lord George Gordon make dat burnin job.
Mine Gote, Yan, mind me, rader lose dy Place,
Dan suffer such dam nasty dam Disgrace.
I tell you true indeed, ver true, dear Yan,
His Majesty be ver goot sort of man;
But ver ver like indeed as oder men,
Dat is, a leetel stubborn now an den.

'Tink, Yan, of dat ver ugly ting, a Wig,
For pot-boy and de pot-girl run der rig.
Boh! filty ting, enough de deffil for scare;
An made perhap of dismal dead man's hair:
I sal not wonders if, dy soul for shock,
A Ghost come seize upon der stolen Lock;
No, fegs! nor wonders if dey come an pull
De Vig vid mush mush fury from dy scull.
Pon som poor Strumpet head perhap dat grow'd,
Dat die of dam disorder, nasty Toad!'

Thus saying, lo! the Fury made retreat,
And left the Lord of Saucepans in a sweat.
Just like King Richard in his tent, John rear'd,
And verily a Man of Woes appear'd.
Now handling his small Pig-tail, 'Now you're here,'
Exclaim'd the Major; 'but not long, I fear:
Perhaps some good may follow this same dream,
And resolution mar this Shaving-scheme.
Curs'd be the Louse that so much mischief bred,
And yields to Barber's Boys the harmless Head:
Curs'd be the Razor-maker; curs'd the prig
Who thought upon that greasy thing, a Wig.
Sure, 'twas some mangy Beast, some scabby Rogue,
Who brought a thing so filthy into vogue.
Had nature meant the scarecrow to be worn,
Infants with Wigs had certainly been *born*;
But, lo! with little Hair, and that uncurl'd,
But not with Wigs, they come into the World.
What shame, that Sheep, that Horses, Cows, and Bulls,
Should club their Tails, to furnish Christian sculls!
But what a sacrilegious shame, the *dead*
Can't keep, poor souls, their Locks upon their head!
What shame the Spectres, in the midnight air,
Should wander, screaming for their plunder'd Hair!
Curs'd be the Shaving-plan, I say again,
Although the bantling of a Royal brain!'

Thus curs'd the Major to Night's listening ear,
Enough to turn a Christian pale to hear:
Thus, heedless of hereafter, for a pin
Will Men and Women run their souls in sin.

Now paus'd the Major, with a thoughtful air;
And now soliloquied with solemn stare:
'Drunk with dominion, gorged with vicious thoughts,
With folly teeming, dozed by flattery's draughts,
Taught to admire their very maudlin dreams,
And think their brains' dull mudpools Wisdom's streams,
Too many a Monarch lives, but, lo! not ours;
A King who Wisdom's very self devours;
Snaps at arts, sciences, where'er they rise,
With all the fire of Boys at Butterflies.
Such cannot, surely, own a *little* heart;
Therefore our Locks and we *may* never part.' –
Now, from a stool, a tinder-box he took,
And fiercely with the stone the steel he struck:
And, after many unsuccessful shocks,
The sparks inflamed the tinder in the box,
Which, by a match which John did sagely handle,
Gave sudden lustre to a farthing candle.
[...]

Now, full illuminated, Dixon stole
Where lay a Master-cook within his hole:
From whence, to all th' inferior Cooks they went,
Inclined to Opposition's big intent;
But not so fierce, alas! for Opposition,
As in the threatening bullying Petition;
For men (it is reported) dash and vapour
Less on the field of battle, than on *paper*.
Thus, in the history of each *dire* campaign,
More carnage loads the Newspaper than Plain.

And now, the Cooks and Scullions left each nest;
And now, behold, they one and all were drest.
Lo! sullen to the Kitchen moved the throng,
Gloom on each eye, and silence on each tongue:
How much like crape-clad Mourners round a Bier!
But, ah! impress'd with sorrow more sincere;
For oft at tombs with joy the *bosom* burns;
There, 'tis the sable *black alone* that mourns. –
Now making, with a few dry chips, a fire,
They sullen sat, their grief commix'd with ire;
Sad ruminating all around the flame,
Like Harry and his Band, of deathless name,

Near Agincourt, expectant of the day
Big with the horrors of a bloody fray;
A fray that threaten'd his poor little Band,
To sweep it, just like Spiders, to that land
Terra incognita yclep'd, which stretches
Afar;– of which, imperfect are our sketches;
Since all who have surveyed this distant bourn,
So welcom'd, were not suffer'd to return.
Thus did the Cooks expect the fatal morn
When, Sheep-like, every Head was to be shorn.

Now to the whitening East they cast their sight,
And wish'd, but vainly, an eternal night.
[…]

Not with less pleasure doth a Poet look
On cruel Criticism, which damns his Book,
Or recommends it to that peaceful shore
Where Books and Bards are never heard of more:–
Than look'd each man, with lengthen'd boding beard,
On that sad morn which doom'd them to be shear'd.
Not with less pleasure, likewise let me say,
A hungry Author sees his dying Play;
Child of his dotage, who surveys its fall,
Just as Mankind shall view the tumbling Ball;
When Sun, Moon, Stars, and all the distant Spheres,
Burst in one general Wreck about their ears.
[…]
Now did the Major hum a tune so sad,
Chromatic, in the robes of sorrow clad;
But, lo! the Ballad could not fear control,
Nor exorcise the Barbers from his soul.
And now his lifted eyes the ceiling sought;
And now he whistled, *not* 'for want of thought.'
A mournful Air the whistling Major chose:
Still on his rolling eye the Razors rose.
From grave to sprightly now he changed, a jig:
Still o'er his haunted fancy waved the Wig;
Still saw his eye alarm'd the Scratch[17] abhorr'd,

---

17 A small Wig, or rather an Apology for a Wig, so called, and generally worn by
   our most amiable and august Monarch.

Like wild Macbeth's the visionary Sword.
[...]

Sing, Muse, (or lo! our *canto* not complete,)
What Air he humm'd, and whistled all so sweet.
Homer of every thing minutely speaks,
From Heaven's Ambrosia to a camp's Beef-steaks:
Then let us, Muse, adopt a march sublime,
And try to rival Homer with our Rhyme;
Who, had a Nit, in Juno's tresses bred,
Dropp'd on divine Minerva's wiser head;
Or Cook-like Flea, exploring some new track,
Hopp'd from the clouds to Agamemnon's back;
The Bard had sung the fall in Verse divine,
And Critics heard the sound along the line.
[...]
The Bard who never wrote an idle word,
Bade his bold Verse the God's bold Speech record:
And had the Thunderer but broke wind, the Song
Had, imitative, borne the Blast along. –
Then be it known to all the World around,
To Folks above, and People under ground,
To Fish and Fowl, and every Creeping Thing,–
Lillibullero, and *God save the King*,
Were actually the very Airs he chose;
But wherefore, God Almighty only knows.

(Canto IV. December 1792)

Canto III, which has introduced personified abstractions instead of the gods, ends with another mockery of epic conventions when the Muse has to recall the tunes that the Major was whistling. Wolcot wrote Canto IV at the end of 1792 to introduce the wives of the cooks, who argue with Secker, a former Clerk of the Kitchens, about the shaving of their husbands' heads. They claim that their husbands are clean and say that the only reason for their shabby treatment is because they are poor. They accuse Secker of being the source of the Louse. This insubordination allows Peter Pindar to insinuate slyly into his text the following reflection:

> Muse, let us pause a moment. Here we see
> A woman, certainly of low degree,
> Reviling folk of elevated station;
> Thus waging war with mild Subordination.
> Should sweet Subordination chance to die,
> Adieu to Kings and Courtier-men so high.

In such a situation, the Queen herself would have to do her own household chores, as the servant class would have disappeared. Prudence prevents Secker from giving vent to his anger and the argument is interrupted by the arrival of the King and his entourage, along with the barber. The King demands that his edict will be obeyed. The royal princesses are on the scene too and these sympathetic English women open Canto V with an appeal to their father for mercy to be shown to the servants. Madame Schwellen-berg, as villain of the piece and representative of despotic Germanic traditions, has the nerve to oppose the princesses, who have the interest of the English servants at heart. The princesses, like the Prince of Wales, read Peter Pindar's works. He presents them with a special compliment, and demonstrates his loyalty to the next generation of the royal family.

from *Canto the Fifth. November 1795*

NOW, with the sweetest Lips that love inspire,
The Princess Royal thus addressed her Sire:
'O Sir, for once attend a Daughter's prayer;
Restrain your fury from your people's Hair:
A thousand blessings will their mouths bestow,
And every heart with gratitude o'erflow.
For *such* a victory, who would give a fig?
Pray, Sir, don't make them wear a nasty Wig.' –
Such sounds, so sweet, nay so divinely broke,
As might have mollified the sturdy Oak,
Were doom'd in vain on Royal ears to fall:
Yet Music drove the Devil out of Saul!
To her the King, with most astonish'd eyes,
And surly wrinkled brow, so stern replies:
'What, what? not shave 'em, shave 'em, now they're *caught*?
What! have this pretty hubbub all for *nought*?
No, no, Girl; no, Girl; no, Girl; no, Girl; no:
Beg on till Doomsday, Girl, it shan't be so.
How, how, pray, would it look; how, how, pray, look?
People would swear I *could not* shave a Cook.
You call Wigs *nasty*, Miss? Fine speech, indeed!
Don't, don't you see I've one upon my head?
Go back, go back, Miss Pert,' he bluntly cried;
Then with his elbow pushed the Nymph aside.
Although he did not box her lovely ears,
He drowned the radiance of her eye with tears.

Far from the wrathful King the Maid withdrew,
And veiled her modest beauties from his view.
[...]
In tears she moves away, the heavenly Maid,
And leaves him Monarch of the mighty Shade.

Now o'er his lofty shoulder, with a sigh,
The fair Augusta cast a pitying eye;
And whispered, ah! so soft, so sweet a prayer,

To save from Razor-rage the heads of Hair!
When lo, the King:
'What, *you* too, Miss, petition for each knave?
You, you too, Miss, an enemy to *shave*?

Mute was the Maid; when lo! with modest looks,
Distressed, she shrunk away from King and Cooks:
Thus, o'er a shouldering Cloud the Moon so bright
Oft gives a peep of momentary light;
Much as to say, 'I wish my smiles to grant,
To cheer you darkling mortals, but I can't.'

Sing, heavenly Goddess, how the Cooks behaved,
Who swore they'd all be damned ere they'd be shaved;
Who penn'd to Majesty the bold Petition,
And daring fumed with rebel Opposition.

Cowed, cowed, alas! the Lords of Saucepans feel;
Each Heart so valorous sunk into the Heel;
And then, each threatening Amazonian Dame,
Her spirit drooping, and extinct her flame:
For lo! of Majesty the powerful Blaze,
His Coat's bright Gold, and Eyeball's rolling Gaze,
Just like the Light that covered sad Saint Paul,
Flashed on their visages, and smote them all. –
Who could have thought that things would thus have ended?
Fate seemingly a dreadful crash intended;
Such stately resolution in the Cooks,
Such fierce demeanour in their Spouses' looks!
But thus in Western India Jove ordains
At times an aspect wild of Hurricanes:
Dark grows the sky, with gleams of threatening red;
All nature dumb, the smallest zephyr dead;
Bird, beast, and mortal, trembling, pausing still,
Expectant of the Tempest's mighty will:
Tremendous pause! when lo, by small degrees,
Light melts the mass; with life returns the breeze;
And Danger, on his cloud, who scowled dismay,
Moves sullen with his threatening glooms away.

There Royalty succeeded; but, alas!
In foreign climes this Gold will scarcely pass.

Sorry am I indeed, and grieved to hear,
That Royalty is falling from its sphere;
War's mighty *first-rate*, dwindling to a *skiff*;
The knees of Adoration waxing stiff,
That bent so pliantly to *folk* of State:
Cock-turkey Grandeur verging to his fate.
But thus exclaims the Mob: 'In folly far,
Folk deemed a Beam from Bogs a Falling Star;
And fancied Thunder, all so dread, ador'd,
The Voice tremendous of an anger'd Lord;
The Lightning his swift Vengeance: never dreaming
That mortals, ever poring, ever scheming,
Should find that in a phial they should lock it,
And bear *Heaven's vengeance* in their Breeches-pocket.
See France: lo! Homage much has lost her awe,
And blushes now to kiss the Lion's paw;
Nay, dares to fancy (an old rebel jade)
Emperors and *Thrones* of *like materials* made;
Nay, fancy too (on bold Rebellion's brink),
That Subjects have a *right* to *speak* and *think*;
Revileth Kings, for praise and wonder born;
Calleth Crowns Fools' Caps, that *their* heads adorn:
And sacred Sceptres, which we *here adore*,
Mean Picklocks for the houses of the poor.
Thus Curiosity no longer springs,
And wide-mouthed Wonder gapes no more at Kings.
Heavens! if Equality all ranks confounds,
No more shall we be whistled to, like Hounds;
Freedom will talk to Kings in dauntless tone,
And Female Majesty be just plain Joan.

Now taking courage, to his honest breast
His hand the Major energetic press'd;
Clothed with humility's mild beam his eye,
He thus address'd the Monarch with a sigh:
'O King! you've call'd me an old fool, to whine:
But I'm not *old*; still many a year is mine.
So white, as though from Time, my temples grow,
Ingratitude's cold hand hath formed their snow:
Grief dims these eyes, and whitens every hair;
And, lo! my wrinkles are the tracks of Care.
To tread Life's wild, unwounded by a thorn,

Was ne'er the lucky lot of woman-born.
Man should be kind to man, O Best of Kings,
And try to blunt the ills that Nature brings;
Not bid the cup of bitterness o'erflow,
And to her thousands add another woe.
Ah! if a *trifle* can a smile employ,
How cruel, Sir, to *kill* the infant joy!
How faint of happiness the scattered ray,
That cheers of life, alas, the little day;
While Care and Sorrow's imp-like host invade,
And fill a sighing universe with shade!
Then bid your noble indignation cease,
And suffer our poor Locks to rest in peace.'

He ended. – Now, with scorn so keen inspired,
And anger, uninvited, undesired,
Did Madame Schwellenberg, devoid of grace,
O'er the Queen's shoulder poke her Cat-like face;
And thus: 'Mine Gote den, vat a saucy vretch!
How cleberly dis poor old fella preach!
Bring him de polepit; dat he sal be pote in:
Jan beat de Mettodisses all as notin.'

Now spoke the Spouse of our *most glorious* King,
Who deemed a Louse a very nasty thing:
For *folk* of *Strelitz* are so neat and clean,
They think on vermin with abhorrent mien;
For cleanliness so much in *Strelitz* thrives,
Folks never saw a Louse in all their lives.
'Mine Gote! 'mong men an women, an de boys,
Dis shave indeed make very pretty noise.
Goote Gote! make rout about a leetel Hair!
Wig be de fashion; Dixon, take de shair:
Sheet down, and don't make hubbub shust like Pig;
Dere's noting terrible about a Wig.
Mine Gote! de tremblin fellow seem afred,
As if we put a Tiger 'pon his head:
De Ladies now wear Wig upon der crown;
So sheet you down, Jan Dixon, sheet you down.
Cook tell his King and Queen he von't be shave?
Egote! de Englis don't know how behave.
Let Cook say so in Strelitz, ah mine Gote!

Dere would be Soldiers dat would cut der troat.
You know dat King an Queen, you rebel Jan,
Can cut your Head off in a moment, man:
Lord! den you may be tankfull dat we *spare*,
An only cut off goote-for-notin Hair.
You know dat in our History you read,
How King of Englond cut off Subject's head.'

Now silence broke the King: 'Sit down, sit down;
Come, come, let every Barber take his crown:
I'll show some mercy t'ye, ye nasty Pigs;
For mind, mind, mind, I'll *pay* for all the Wigs.'

At these last words, forth crawled an ancient Dame,
Sharp-nosed, half-starved, and Avarice her name;
With wrinkled Neck and Parchment-like to view,
That e'en the coarsest kerchief seldom knew;
With Hawk-like Eyes that glisten'd o'er her gold,
And raptured every hour her treasure told;
Who of her Fingers form'd a Comb so fair,
And with a Garter Filleted her hair;
Who fiercely snatch'd, with wild devouring eyes,
An atom of Brown Sugar from the Flies;
Made a sad Candle from a dab of Fat,
And stole a stinking Fish-head from a Cat;
Saves of the mustiest Bread the Crumbs, and sees
A Dinner in the *scrapings* of a Cheese.
Whiffing a stump of Pipe, a frequent treat,
That gives the stomach Smoke, poor thing! for Meat,
Forth hobbled this old Dame, with shaking head,
Like, in her crooked Form, the letter Z;
The Palace-watch, and Guardian most severe
Of drops of dying and of dead Small-beer:
A Dame who hated idle dogs and cats,
And trembled at a rumpus of the rats;
Nay, listen'd, jealous of a scratching *mouse*,
Afraid the imp might *swallow* the *whole house*:
The province hers, to sell old palace-shoes,
Old hats, old coats, and breeches, to the Jews;
And drive, with Dog-like fury, from the door,
The plaintive murmurs of the famish'd poor.
[...]

Forth hobbled she; and, in a quick shrill tone,
Thus to the King of Nations spoke the Crone:

'God bless us, Sir; why give me leave to say,
Your Majesty is throwing things away.
What! *give* the fellows Wigs for every head?
A piece of rare extravagance indeed!
Let them *buy* Wigs *themselves*, a dirty Crew:
An't please your Majesty, what's that to you?
You buy the rascals Wigs indeed, so nice!
It only *gives encouragement* to Lice.
Marry come up indeed, I say; new Wigs!
No: let them *suffer* for't, the nasty Pigs.
Lord! they can well afford it: Sir, their Hair
Costs (Heaven protect us!) what would make you stare.
Hours in the Barber's hands, forsooth, they sit
Reading the newspapers, and books of wit;
Just like our Men of Quality, forsooth,
Each full-aged gentleman, and dapper youth;
Newmarket now, and now the *Nation*, studying,
In clouds of Flour sufficient for a Pudding.
Lord, what extravagance I see and hear!
Unlike your Majesty, and Madam there,
Our Great consume and squander, fling away:
'Tis rout and hubbub; spend, spend, night and day.
Such racketing, that people's peace destroys;
As if the world was only made for noise.
Would every Duchess copy our good Queen,
More money in their purses would be seen.
Her Majesty to things can condescend,
Which our fine Quality, with nose on end,
Behold with *such* contempt, and *such* a grin,
As though a little Saving was a Sin.
Her Majesty, God bless her! does not scorn
To see a stocking and a shoe *well worn*;
To mend, or darn, or clean, a lutestring gown,
So mock'd indeed by all the Great in town.
Her Majesty at Frogmore,[18] day and night,

---

18 A Farm near Windsor, where a parcel of young Women, the *protégées* of Majesty,
are constantly employed in working beds, and very well know the meaning of
the phrase, 'Working one's fingers to the stumps.'

Can to their labour keep her Pupils tight;
See that to Milliners no trifle goes,
That may be done beneath *her own* great nose.
Her Majesty can buy a hat, or cloak,
In shops, indeed, as cheap as *common folk*:
She will not be imposed upon, she says;
Oh what a good example for *our* days!
When Prudence dictates, lo! no pride she feels:
Could order shoes to come with *copper* heels.
Yes, Majesty could nobly *pride* renounce,
And make a handsome *jacket* of a *flounce*;
'Stead *of lawn gauze*, descend to humble *crape*;
And, 'stead of *ribbon*, draw a gown with *tape*;
Turn hats to bonnets, by her prudence led,
And clean a tarnish'd spangled shoe with bread;
A gown's worn sleeve from *long* to *short* devote,
And into pockets cut an upper coat;
Cut shifts to night-caps, satin cloaks to muffs,
And calmly frill groat ribbons into ruffs:
Blest with the rarest economic wits,
Transform an old silk stocking into *mits*;
Transform too (so convertible are things)
E'en flannel petticoats to caps for Kings.
And then *your* Majesty, whom God long keep;
How fond indeed of every thing that's *cheap*!
'Best is best cheap,' you very wisely cry;
And so, an't please your Majesty, say I.
Lord bless us! why should people spend and riot,
When people can *so save* by living quiet?
Give to the *poor*, forsooth? a rare exploit!
Catch what you can, and never *give* a doit.
To Saving, every one should go to school:
To my mind, Generosity's a fool.
Give, Sir, no Wigs to Cooks; for, as I say,
'Tis kindness and good money flung away.'

Thus ended Avarice, at last, her Speech;
With praise of King, and Queen, and Saving, rich.
Such words, delivered with a solemn air,
Gave to the King of Men's great eye a stare.
'Right, right, 'tis very right,' the Monarch cries,
And on his millions rolls his mental eyes:

'Right, Mistress Avarice; right, right, indeed;
I won't buy Wigs for every nasty Head.
No, no; they'll save it, save it, as you say:
I won't, I won't, I won't fling pence away.'

Here let us pause again, and think how hard
That good intentions should be quickly marr'd.
Ah! Generosity's a tender plant,
Its root so weakly, and its bearings scant.
Self-love, too near it, robs it of each ray,
And thirsty sucks the rills of life away;
Vile Weed (like Docks, in coarsest soil which start)
That thriveth in the cold and flinty heart.

'Come, come, sit down' the Monarch deign'd to rave;
'Cooks, Cooks, sit down. Come, Barbers, shave, shave, shave.
Yes, yes, I think 'tis right, 'tis right and just:
Indeed you must be shaved; you must, you must.
Cooks must not over their Superiors tower:
We must, must show the World that we have power.'
[...]
Now to the Cooks, O wandering Muse, return,
For, lo! our Readers with impatience burn.
Awed by the voice of King, and Queen, and Page,
And Madame Schwellenberg's relentless rage,
Down sat the Cooks, amid a wondering host;
The Barbers laboured, – and the Locks were lost! –
[...]

Speak, heavenly Goddess; was there then no Fray,
No drops of Blood effused to mark the day?
No fisticuffs, no Eyes as black as Night,
No Cat-like scratches, no revengeful bite? –
Nor fisticuffs, nor Eyes as black as Night,
Nor Cat-like scratches, nor revengeful bite,
The Palace witness'd. Thus the Muse divine
Must close, without one drop of Blood, the line;
And Readers, baulk'd of deeds of high renown,
Perhaps shall, grumbling for their money, frown.
What can we do, if Fate produced *no* fray?
The Poet dares not *make* a murderous day.
Should Falsehood's tale my sacred Song defile,

Which damneth half th' historians of our isle;
How could I hold aloft my tuneful head,
Or proudly hope at Doomsday to be read;
The glowing wish of every Son of Rhyme,
To live a favourite to the end of time?
Yet nought were easier than to *form* a Fray,
And bring a dozen Gods to aid the day:
Yet nought were easier than to raise a Battle;
Make iron head-piece against head-piece rattle;
Nails nails oppose, and grinders grinders greet,
Nose poke at nose, and stomachs stomachs meet;
Wild-rolling eye-balls against eye-balls glare;
The dusty floor be strewed with teeth and hair;
Caps, petticoats, and kerchiefs, load the ground;
The trembling roofs with mingled cries resound;
Legs of joint-stools, and chairs, their vengeance pour;
And blocks and mopsticks fly, a wooden show'r;
Raise Clamours equal to an Indian Yell,
Transcended only by the Cries of Hell;
And bid old Erebus, in sulphur strong,
Display his flaming cauldron in our song. –

Proud of the *shave*, the King of Nations smil'd;
Nay, laugh'd triumphant, with his glory wild.
But still, to show his *justice*, thus he said:

'Mind, mind me, Gentry with the Shaven Head;
Know, know, the Louse belongs to some of *you*:
It is a Louse, it is; 'tis very true:
Yes, yes, belongs to some one of the house;
I've read Buffon; yes, yes, I know a Louse.'
A pill-box then he oped, with eager look,
And showed the Crawler, to convince each Cook. –
The long-eared Beast of Balaam, lo, we find,
Sharp to the *beast* that rode him spoke his mind:
The mournful Xanthus[19] (says the Bard of old),
Of Peleus' warlike Son the fortune told:
Thus to the captive Louse was language given;
Which *proves* what interest Justice holds in Heaven.

19 The Horse of Achilles.

The Vermin, rising on his little rump,
Like Ladies' Lap-dogs that for muffin mump,
Thus, solemn as our Bishops *when* they preach,
Made to the Best of Kings his *maiden* Speech:

'Know, mighty Monarch, I was born and bred
Deep in the burrows of a Page's head;
There took I sweet *Lousilla* unto Wife,
My soul's delight, the comfort of my life:
But on a day, your Page, Sir, dared invade
Cowslip's sweet lips, your faithful Dairy-maid;
Great was the struggle for the short-lived bliss,
At length he won the long-contested Kiss:
When, 'mid the struggle, thus it came to pass;
Down dropp'd my Wife and I upon the Lass;
From whence we crawled (and who's without ambition?
Who does not wish to *better* his condition?)
To *you*, dread Sir; where, lo, we loved and fed,
Charmed with the fortune of a *greater* Head;
Where, safe from nail and comb, and blustering wind,
We nestled in your little Lock behind;
Where many a beauteous Baby plainly proves,
Heaven, like a King's, can bless a Louse's loves;
Where many a time, at Court I've joined your Grace,
And with you gallop'd in the glorious chase;
Lousilla too, my Children, and my Nits,
Just frighten'd sometimes out of all their wits.
It happen'd, Sir (ah luckless, luckless day!),
I foolish took it in my head to stray:
(How many a father, mother, daughter, son,
Are oft by Curiosity undone!)
Dire wish! for, 'midst my travels, urged by Fate,
From You, O King, I fell upon your Plate.
Sad was the Precipice; and now I'm here,
Far from Lousilla and my Children dear;
[...]
Thus, Sir, are you mistaken all this while,
And Queen and Pages that our race revile;
As though our species could not life *adorn*,
And that th' Almighty made a Louse in *scorn*.
Yet, if to Genealogy we go,
The Louse is of the *elder house*, I trow.

Ere God (so Moses says[20]) did Man create;
Lo, our first Parents walked the World in *state*. –
Such is the history of your loyal Louse,
Whose presence breeds such tumult in the house:
Thus, Sir, you see no blame to Cooks belong;
Thus Majesty, for *once*, is in the wrong.'

Thus, in the manly tones of Fox and Pitt,
To George intrepid spoke the Son of Nit:
Firm in his language to the King of wrath,
As little David to the Man of Gath;
Ordain'd, in oratory, to surpass
The Speech, th' immortal Speech, of Balaam's Ass.

'Lies, lies, lies, lies!' replied the furious King;
''Tis no such thing: no, no, 'tis no such thing.'
Then quick he aim'd, of red-hot anger full,
His nails of vengeance at the Louse's scull.
But Zephyr, anxious for his life, drew near,
And sudden bore him to a distant sphere;
In triumph raised the Animal on high,
Where Berenice's Locks[21] adorn the Sky;
But now he wished him *nobler* fame to share,
And crawl for ever on Belinda's[22] Hair.
Yet to the Louse was *greater* glory given;
To roll a Planet on the splendid Heaven,
And draw of deep Astronomers the ken,
The *Georgium Sidus*[23] of the Sons of Men.

20 The Louse shows great Biblical knowledge.
21 [Berenice was the wife of King Ptolemy of Egypt. According to legend, her hair was placed among the stars as a constellation.]
22 [Belinda was the heroine of Alexander Pope's *Rape of the Lock*.]
23 [The King's friend, the astronomer Sir William Herschel, discovered the planet Uranus in 1781. His original name for it was 'George's Star' – Georgium Sidus – but other astronomers, in Europe and elsewhere, disapproved of the discovery being linked with the British king and the name was eventually changed to Uranus.]

Tales of the King

from *An Apologetic Postscript to Ode upon Ode.*
1787

What *modern* Courtier, pray, hath got the face
To say to Majesty, 'O King!
At *such* a time, in *such* a place,
You did a very foolish thing?'
What Courtier, not a foe to his own glory,
Would publish of his King *this* simple Story? –

The Apple Dumplings and a King

ONCE on a time, a Monarch, tired with whooping,
Whipping and spurring,
Happy in worrying
A poor, defenceless, harmless Buck
(The Horse and Rider wet as muck),
From his high consequence and wisdom stooping,
Enter'd, through curiosity, a cot
Where sat a poor Old Woman and her pot.

The wrinkled, blear-eyed, good old Granny,
In this same cot, illumed by many a cranny,
Had finish'd Apple-dumplings for her pot:
In tempting row the naked Dumplings lay,
When, lo! the Monarch, in his *usual* way,
Like Lightning spoke: 'What's this? what's this? what? what?'

Then, taking up a Dumpling in his hand,
His eyes with admiration did expand,
And oft did Majesty the Dumpling grapple:
''Tis monstrous, monstrous hard indeed,' he cried:
'What makes it, pray, so hard? – The Dame replied,
Low curtseying, 'Please your Majesty, the Apple.' –

'Very astonishing indeed! strange thing!'
(Turning the Dumpling round, rejoined the King).
''Tis most extraordinary then, all this is;
It beats Pinetti's conjuring all to pieces:
Strange I should never of a Dumpling dream!
But, Goody, tell me where, where, where's the Seam?' –

'Sir, there's no Seam,' quoth she; 'I never knew
That folks did Apple-dumplings *sew*.' –
'No!' cried the staring Monarch with a grin:
'How, how the devil got the Apple in?'

On which the Dame the curious scheme revealed
By which the Apple lay so sly concealed;
Which made the Solomon of Britain start:
Who to the Palace with full speed repaired,
And Queen and Princesses so beauteous scared,
All with the wonders of the Dumpling Art.

There did he labour one whole week, to show
The wisdom of an Apple-dumpling Maker;
And, lo! so deep was Majesty in dough,
The Palace seemed the lodging of a Baker.

*

Reader, thou likest not my Tale; look'st *blue*:
Thou art a Courtier; roarest, 'Lies, lies, lies!' –
Do, for a moment, stop thy cries:
I tell thee, roaring Infidel, 'tis *true*.
[…]
Far from despising Kings, I like the breed,
Provided *king-like* they behave:
Kings are an instrument we need;
Just as we Razors want, to shave;
To keep the State's Face smooth; give it an air
Like my Lord North's, so jolly, round, and fair.

My sense of Kings though freely I impart,
I hate not Royalty; Heaven knows my heart.
Princes and Princesses I like, so loyal:
Great George's Children are my great delight;
The sweet Augusta, and sweet Princess Royal,
Obtain my love by day, and prayers by night.

Yes, I like Kings: and oft look back with pride
Upon the Edwards, Harries, of our isle;
Great souls, in virtue as in valour tried,
Whose Actions bid the cheek of Britons smile.

Muse, let us also *forward* look,
And take a peep into Fate's book.

Behold, the sceptre Young Augustus sways!
I hear the mingled praise of millions rise:
I see upraised to Heaven their ardent eyes,
That for their Monarch ask a length of days.

Bright in the brightest annals of renown,
Behold fair Fame his youthful temples crown
With Laurels of unfading bloom;
Behold Dominion swell beneath his care,
And Genius, rising from a dark despair,
His long-extinguish'd fires relume!

Such are the Kings that suit *my* taste, I own:
Not those where all the *littlenesses* join;
Whose souls should start to find their lot a Throne,
And blush to show their noses on a Coin.

Reader, for fear of wicked applications,
I now allude to Kings of *foreign nations.*

Poets (so unimpeached Tradition says)
The sole Historians were of ancient days;
Who help'd their Heroes, Fame's high hill to clamber:
Penning their glorious acts in language strong;
And thus preserving, by immortal Song,
Their names amidst their tuneful Amber.

What am *I* doing? Lord! the very same:
Preserving many a deed deserving fame,
Which that old lean devouring Shark called Time
Would without ceremony eat;
In my opinion, far too rich a treat.
I therefore merit *statues* for my Rhyme.

'All this is laudable,' a Quaker cries;
But let grave Wisdom, Friend, thy Verses rule;
Put out thine Irony's two squinting eyes;
Despise thy grinning Monkey, Ridicule.' –

What! slight my sportive Monkey, Ridicule,
Who acts like Birch on Boys at School,
Neglecting lessons, truant perhaps whole weeks!
My Ridicule, with humour fraught and wit,
Is that *satiric* friend, a Gouty Fit,
Which *bites* men into Health and rosy Cheeks;
[…]

from *Instructions to a Celebrated Laureat*

Birth-Day Ode (Alias Mr Whitbread's Brewhouse). May 1787

THIS day, this very day, gave birth
Not to the *brightest* Monarch upon earth,
Because there are *some* brighter, and as big;
Who love the Arts that Man exalt to Heaven:
George loves them also, when they're given
To four-legg'd Gentry, christened Dog and Pig,[24]
Whose deeds in this our wonder-hunting Nation
Prove what a charming thing is *education.*

Full of the art of Brewing Beer,
The Monarch heard of Mister Whitbread's fame:
Quoth he unto the Queen, 'My dear, my dear,
Whitbread hath got a marvellous great name.
Charly, we must, must, must see Whitbread brew;
Rich as us, Charly; richer than a Jew.
Shame, shame, we have not yet his Brewhouse seen.' –
Thus *sweetly* said the King unto the Queen.

Red-hot with Novelty's delightful rage,
To Mister Whitbread forth he sent a Page,
To say that Majesty proposed to view,
With thirst of Knowledge deep inflamed,
His vats, and tubs, and hops, and hogsheads famed,
And learn the *noble* secret, how to *brew.*

Of such undreamt of *honour* proud,
Most reverently the Brewer bow'd;
So humbly (so the humble story goes),
He touch'd e'en *terra firma* with his nose:

24 The Dancing Dogs and Wise Pig have formed a considerable part of the Royal
 Amusement.

Then said unto the Page, hight Billy Ramus,
'Happy are we that our great King should name us,
As worthy unto Majesty to shew
How we poor Chiswell people *brew*.'

Away sprung Billy Ramus, quick as Thought:
To Majesty the *welcome* tidings brought;
How Whitbread staring stood like any Stake,
And trembled: then the civil things he said:
On which the King did smile, and nod his head;
For Monarchs like to see their Subjects *quake*.

Such *horrors* unto Kings most *pleasant* are,
Proclaiming reverence and humility;
High thoughts too all those shaking fits declare
Of kingly Grandeur and *great* Capability.

People of worship, wealth, and birth,
Look on the humbler Sons of Earth
Indeed in a most humble light, God knows.
High Stations are like Dover's towering Cliffs,
Where Ships below appear like little Skiffs;
The People walking on the strand, like Crows.

Muse, sing the stir that Mister Whitbread made;
Poor gentleman, most terribly afraid
He should not charm enough his Guests *divine*:
He gave his Maids new aprons, gowns, and smocks;
And, lo! Two hundred pounds were spent in frocks,
To make th' Apprentices and Draymen fine.

Busy as Horses in a field of clover,
Dogs, cats, and chairs, and stools, were tumbled over,
Amidst the Whitbread rout of preparation
To treat the lofty Ruler of the Nation.

Now moved King, Queen, and Princesses, so grand,
To visit the first Brewer in the land;
Who sometimes swills his beer and grinds his meat
In a snug corner christen'd Chiswell-street;
But oftener, charm'd with *fashionable* air,
Amidst the gaudy Great of Portman-square.

Lord Aylesbury, and Denbigh's Lord *also,*
His Grace the Duke of Montague *likewise,*
With Lady Harcourt, joined the Raree-show,
And fixed all Smithfield's marvelling eyes:
For, lo! A greater *show* ne'er graced those quarters,
Since Mary roasted, just like Crabs, the Martyrs.

Arrived, the King broad-grinn'd, and gave a nod
To Mister Whitbread; who, had God
Come with his Angels to behold his beer,
With more respect he never could have met:
Indeed the man was in a sweat,
So much the Brewer did the King revere.

Her Majesty *contrived* to make a dip:
Light as a Feather then the King did skip;
And ask'd a thousand Questions, with a laugh,
Before poor Whitbread comprehended *half.*

Reader, my Ode should have a Simile:
Well, in Jamaica, on a Tamarind-tree,
Five hundred Parrots, gabbling just like Jews,
I've seen; such noise the feather'd imps did make
As made my pericranium ache,
Asking and telling parrot-news.

Thus was the Brewhouse fill'd with gabbling noise,
While Draymen, and the Brewer's Boys,
Devoured the Questions that the King did ask:
In different parties were they staring seen,
Wondering to think they saw a *King* and *Queen;*
Behind a tub were some, and some behind a cask.

Some Draymen forced themselves (a pretty luncheon)
Into the mouth of many a gaping puncheon;
And through the bung-hole wink'd with curious eye,
To view, and be assured, what sort of things
Were Princesses, and Queens, and Kings,
For whose most lofty station thousands sigh.
And, lo! Of all the gaping Puncheon clan,
Few were the Mouths that had not got a Man.

Now Majesty into a Pump so deep
Did with an opera-glass of Dollond peep,
Examining with care each wondrous matter
That brought up water.

Thus have I seen a Magpie in the street,
A chattering Bird we often meet,
A Bird for curiosity well known,
With head awry,
And cunning eye,
Peep knowingly into a Marrow-bone.

And now his curious Majesty did stoop,
To count the nails on every hoop;
And, lo! no single thing came in his way,
That, full of deep research, he did not say,
'What's this? hæ, hæ? what's that? What's this? what's that?'
So quick the words too, when he deign'd to speak,
As if each Syllable would break its Neck.

Thus, to the world of *great* while others crawl,
Our Sovereign peeps into the world of *small*:
Thus microscopic Geniuses explore
Things that too oft provoke the public scorn;
Yet swell of useful knowledges the store,
By finding Systems in a Pepper-corn.

Now Mister Whitbread serious did declare,
To make the Majesty of England stare,
That he had Butts enough, he knew,
Placed side by side, to reach along to Kew.
On which the King with wonder swiftly cried,
'What, if they reach to Kew then side by side,
What would they do, what, what, placed end to end?'
To whom, with knitted calculating brow,
The Man of Beer most solemnly did vow,
Almost to Windsor that they would extend.

On which the King, with wondering mien,
Repeated it unto the wondering Queen:

On which, quick turning round his halter'd head,
The Brewer's Horse with face astonish'd neigh'd;
The Brewer's Dog too pour'd a note of thunder,
Rattled his chain, and wagg'd his tail for wonder.

Now did the King for *other* Beers inquire,
For Calvert's, Jordan's, Thrale's entire;
And, after talking of these different Beers,
Asked Whitbread if *his* Porter *equall'd theirs*.

This was a puzzling, disagreeing Question;
Grating like Arsenic on his Host's digestion:
A kind of question to the Man of Cask,
That not even Solomon himself would ask.

Now Majesty, alive to knowledge, took
A very pretty Memorandum-book,
With gilded leaves of asses' skin so white,
And in it legibly began to write:–
                    Memorandum.
A charming place beneath the Grates,
For roasting Chesnuts or *Potates*.
                    Mem.
'Tis Hops that give a bitterness to Beer:
Hops grow in Kent, says Whitbread, and elsewhere.
                    Quære.
Is there no *cheaper* stuff? where doth it dwell?
Would not Horse-aloes bitter it as well?
                    Mem.
To try it soon on our Small-beer;
'Twill *save* us several pounds a year.
                    Mem.
To *remember* to *forget* to ask
Old Whitbread to my house one day.
                    Mem.
Not to *forget* to take of Beer the Cask,
The Brewer offer'd me, away. –

Now having pencil'd his Remarks so shrewd,
Sharp as the Point indeed of a new Pin;
His Majesty his watch most sagely view'd,
And then put up his asses' skin.

To Whitbread now deign'd Majesty to say,
'Whitbread, are all your Horses fond of Hay?'
'Yes, please your Majesty,' in humble notes
The Brewer answer'd: 'also, Sir, of Oats.
Another thing my Horses too maintains;
And that, an't please your Majesty, are Grains.'

'Grains, grains,' said Majesty, 'to fill their crops?
Grains, grains? That comes from hops; yes, hops, hops, hops.'

Here was the King, like Hounds sometimes, *at fault*.
'Sire,' cried the humble Brewer, 'give me leave
Your sacred Majesty to undeceive:
Grains, Sire, are never made from Hops, but Malt.'

'True,' said the cautious Monarch with a smile:
'From malt, malt, malt: I meant malt all the while.' –
'Yes,' with the sweetest bow rejoined the Brewer,
'An't please your Majesty, you did, I'm sure.' –
'Yes,' answered Majesty with quick reply,
'I did, I did, I did, I, I, I, I.'

Now this was *wise* in Whitbread; here we find
A very pretty knowledge of mankind:
As Monarchs never must be in the *wrong*,
'Twas really a bright thought in Whitbread's tongue,
To tell a little fib or some such thing,
To save the sinking credit of a King.

Some Brewers, in the rage of information,
Proud to instruct the Ruler of a Nation,
Had on the folly dwelt, to seem damn'd clever.
Now what had been the consequence? Too plain,
The man had cut his *consequence* in twain;
The King had hated the *wise* Fool for ever.

Reader, whene'er thou dost espy a Nose
That bright with many a Ruby glows;
That Nose, thou mayst pronounce, nay safely swear,
Is nursed on something better than Small-beer:

Thus, when thou findest Kings in *brewing* wise,
Or Natural History holding lofty station;
Thou mayst conclude with marvelling eyes,
Such Kings have had a *goodly* education.

Now did the King admire the Bell so fine,
That daily asks the Draymen all to dine;
On which the Bell rung out (how very proper!),
To show it *was* a Bell, and had a Clapper.

And now before their Sovereign's curious eye,
Parents and Children, fine fat hopeful sprigs,
All snuffling, squinting, grunting, in their sty,
Appear'd the Brewer's tribe of handsome Pigs:
On which th'observant Man who fills a Throne,
Declared the Pigs were vastly like his own:

On which the Brewer, swallowed up in joys,
Tears and astonishment in both his eyes,
His soul brimful of sentiments so loyal,
Exclaimed: 'O Heavens! And can *my* Swine
Be deemed by Majesty so fine?
Heavens! Can *my* Pigs compare, Sire, with Pigs Royal?'
To which the King assented with a nod:
On which the Brewer bowed, and said, 'Good God!'
Then wink'd significant on Miss,
Significant of wonder and of bliss;
Who, bridling in her chin divine,
Cross'd her fair hands, a dear Old Maid,
And then her lowest curtsey made
For such *high honour* done her Father's Swine.

Now did his Majesty so gracious say
To Mister Whitbread, in his flying way,
'Whitbread, d'ye *nick* th' Excisemen now and then?
Hæ, Whitbread, when d'ye think to leave off trade?
Hæ, what? Miss Whitbread's still a Maid, a Maid?
What, what's the matter with the Men?

'D'ye hunt? hæ, hunt? No, no, you are too old.
You'll be Lord May'r, Lord May'r one day;
Yes, yes, I've heard so; yes, yes, so I'm told:

71

Don't, don't the *fine* for Sheriff pay;
I'll prick you every year, man, I declare:
Yes, Whitbread, yes, yes; you shall be Lord May'r.

'Whitbread, d'ye keep a Coach, or job one, pray?
Job, job, that's cheapest; yes, that's best, that's best.
You put your *liveries* on the *Draymen*, hæ?
Hæ, Whitbread, you have feather'd well your nest.
What, what's the price now, hæ, of all your stock?
But, Whitbread, what's o'clock, pray, what's o'clock?'

Now Whitbread inward said, 'May I be curst
If I know *what* to answer *first;*'
Then search'd his brains with ruminating eye:
But ere the Man of Malt an answer found,
Quick on his heel, lo, Majesty turn'd round,
Skipp'd off, and baulk'd the *pleasure* of *reply.* –

Kings in inquisitiveness should be strong;
From curiosity doth wisdom flow:
For 'tis a maxim I've adopted long,
The more a man *inquires*, the more he'll *know*.

Reader, didst ever see a Waterspout?
'Tis possible that thou wilt answer 'No.'
Well then, he makes a most infernal rout;
Sucks, like an Elephant, the waves below,
With huge Proboscis reaching from the sky,
As if he meant to drink the Ocean dry.
At length, so full he can't hold one drop more,
He bursts: down rush the Waters with a roar
On some poor boat, or sloop, or brig, or ship,
And almost sink the Wanderer of the Deep.

Thus have I seen a Monarch, at Reviews,
Suck from the tribe of Officers the news,
Then bear in triumph off each *wondrous* matter,
And souse it on the Queen with *such* a clatter!

I always would advise folks to ask questions;
For truly, Questions are the Keys of Knowledge:
Soldiers who forage for the Mind's digestions,

Cut figures at th' Old Bailey, and at College;
Make Chancellors, Chief Justices, and Judges,
E'en of the lowest Green-bag Drudges.

The Sages say, Dame Truth delights to dwell
(Strange Mansion!) in the bottom of a Well:
Questions are then the Windlass and the Rope
That pull the grave old Gentlewoman up.
Damn jokes then, and unmannerly suggestions,
Reflecting upon Kings for asking Questions.[25] –

Now having well employed his Royal lungs
On nails, hoops, staves, pumps, barrels and their bungs,
The King and Co. sat down to a Collation
Of flesh, and fish, and fowl, of every Nation.

Dire was the clang of plates, of Knife and Fork,
That merciless fell like Tomahawks to work;
And fearless *scalp'd* the fowl, the fish, and cattle,
While Whitbread in the rear beheld the battle.

The *conquering* Monarch, stopping to take breath
Amidst the Regiments of Death,
Now turn'd to Whitbread with complacence round,
And merry thus address'd the Man of Beer:
'Whitbread, is't true? I hear, I hear
You're of an ancient family renown'd.
What, what? I'm told that you're a limb
Of Pym, the famous fellow Pym:[26]
What, Whitbread, is it true what people say?
Son of a Roundhead are you? hæ, hæ, hæ?

'I'm told that you send Bibles to your Votes,
A snuffling Roundheaded Society;
Prayer-books, instead of Cash to buy them coats;
Bunyans, and Practices of Piety:

25 This alludes to the late Dr Johnson's laugh on a Great Personage, for a laudable
    curiosity in the Queen's Library some years since.
26 His Majesty here made a mistake – Pym was his Wife's relation.

73

'Your Bedford Votes would wish to *change their fare*;
Rather see Cash – yes, yes – than Books of Pray'r.
Thirtieth of January don't you *feed*?
Yes, yes; you eat Calf's Head, you eat Calf's Head.'

Now having *wonders* done on flesh, fowl, fish,
Whole *hosts* o'erturn'd, and seized on all supplies;
The Royal Visitors express'd a wish
To turn to House of Buckingham their eyes:

But first the Monarch, so polite,
Ask'd Mister Whitbread if he'd be a *Knight*. –
Unwilling in the list to be enroll'd,
Whitbread contemplated the Knights of Peg,
Then to his *generous* Sovereign made a leg,
And said, he was afraid he was *too old*.
He thank'd however his most gracious King,
For offering to make him *such a Thing*.

But, ah! A different reason 'twas, I fear:
It was not *age* that bade the Man of Beer
The proffer'd *honour* of the Monarch shun;
The tale of Margaret's Knife, and Royal Fright,
Had almost made him damn the *name* of Knight,
A tale that farrowed such a world of Fun.

He mock'd the Prayer too by the King appointed,
Even by himself the Lord's Anointed:[27]
A foe to *fast* too is he, let me tell ye;
And, though a Presbyterian, cannot think
Heaven (quarrelling with meat and drink)
Joys in the grumble of a hungry belly.

Now from the table with Cesarean air
Up rose the Monarch with his *laurel'd* brow;
When Mister Whitbread, waiting on his chair,
Express'd much thanks, much joy, and made a Bow.

---

27 For the *miraculous* escape from a poor innocent insane woman, who only held
out a small Knife in a piece of white paper for her Sovereign to *view*.

Miss Whitbread now so quick her Curtseys drops,
Thick as her *honour'd* Father's Kentish Hops:
Which hop-like curtseys were return'd by Dips
That never hurt the Royal knees and hips;
For hips and knees of Queens are sacred things,
That only bend on gala days
Before the Best of Kings,
When Odes of Triumph sound his praise.

Now through a thundering peal of kind Huzzas,
Proceeding some from hired and *un*hired jaws,[28]
The Raree-show thought proper to retire;
While Whitbread and his Daughter fair
Survey'd all Chiswell-street with lofty air,
For, lo! They felt themselves some *six feet higher.*
[...]
Now God preserve all wonder-hunting Kings,
Whether at Windsor, Buckingham or Kew-house;
And may they *never* do *more foolish* things
Than visiting Sam Whitbread and his Brewhouse!

28 When his Majesty goes to a Play-house, or Brew-house, or Parliament, the Lord
Chamberlain provides some pounds-worth of Mob to huzza their beloved
Monarch. At the Play-house, about forty wide-mouthed fellows are hired on the
night of their Majesties' appearance, at two shillings and sixpence *per* head, with
the liberty of seeing the play *gratis*. These Stentors are placed in different parts
of the Theatre, who, immediately on the Royal entry into the stage-box, set up
their Howl of *loyalty*; to whom their Majesties, with sweetest smiles, acknowl-
edge the *obligation* by a genteel bow, and an elegant curtsey. This congratulatory
noise of the Stentors is looked on by many, particularly Country Ladies and
Gentlemen, as an *infallible* Thermometer that ascertains the *warmth* of the
National Regard.

from *Peter's Pension. 1788*

A SOLEMN EPISTLE TO A SUBLIME PERSONAGE

'My heart is inditing of a good matter: I speak of the things
which I have made, unto the King.' Psalm XLV
Non possum Tecum vivere, nec sine Te.[29]

The Royal Sheep

SOME time ago a dozen Lambs,
Two reverend patriarchal Rams,
And one good motherly old Ewe,
Died on a sudden down at Kew;

Where, with the sweetest innocence, alas!
Those pretty inoffensive Lambs,
And reverend horned patriarchal Rams,
And motherly old Ewe, were nibbling grass:
All the fair property of our great King,
Whose deaths did much the Royal bosom wring.

'Twas said that Dogs had tickled them to death;
Play'd with their gentle throats, and stopp'd their breath.

Like Homer's Heroes on th' ensanguin'd plain,
Stalk'd Mister Robinson[30] around the slain,
And never was more frighten'd in his life.
So shock'd was Mister Robinson's whole face,
Not stronger horrors could have taken place
Had Cerberus devour'd his Wife.

---

29 ['I can live neither with you, nor without you.' Martial, borrowed from Ovid.]
30 The Hind [herdsman].

With wild despairing looks and sighs,
And wet and pity-asking eyes,
He trembling to the Royal presence ventur'd,
White as the whitest Napkin when he enter'd;
White as the Man who sought King Priam's bed,
And told him that his warlike Son was dead.

'Oh! please your Majesty,' he blubb'ring cried;
And then stopp'd short. –
'What? what? what? what?' the staring King replied:
'Speak, Robinson, speak, speak; what, what's the hurt?'

'O Sire,' said Robinson again. –
'Speak,' said the King; 'put, put me out of pain:
Don't, don't in this suspense a body keep.' –
'O Sire,' cried Robinson, 'the Sheep, the Sheep!' –

'What of the Sheep,' replied the King, 'pray, pray?
Dead, Robinson? dead, dead; or run away?' –
'Dead!' answer'd Robinson; 'dead! dead! dead! dead!'
Then, like a drooping Lily, hung his head.

'How? how?' the Monarch ask'd, with visage sad. –
'By Dogs,' said Robinson, 'and likely mad.' –
'No, no, they can't be mad, they can't be mad:
No, no, things arn't so bad, things arn't so bad,'
Rejoin'd the King:
'Off with them quick to *market*; quick, depart;
In with them, in, in with them in a cart:
Sell, sell them for as much as they will bring.'

Now to Fleet Market, driving like the Wind,
Amidst the murder'd Mutton rode the Hind[31]
All in the Royal cart so great,
To try to sell the Royal meat.

The news of this rare batch of Lambs,
And Ewe and Rams,
Design'd for many a London dinner,
Reach'd the fair ears of Master Sheriff Skinner;

31 Mr Robinson.

Who, with a hammer, and a conscience clear,
Gets glory, and ten thousand pounds a year;
And who, if things go tolerably fair,
Will be one day proud London's proud Lord Mayor.

The Alderman was in his pulpit shining,
'Midst Gentlemen with night-caps, hair, and wigs;
In language most rhetorical defining
The sterling merit of a Lot of Pigs:
When suddenly the news was brought,
That in Fleet Market were unwholesome Sheep;
Which made the Preacher from his pulpit leap
As nimble as a Taylor, or as Thought.

For justice panting, and unawed by fears,
This King, this Emperor, of Auctioneers,
Set off: a furious face indeed he put on.
Like Lightning did he gallop up Cheapside,
Like Thunder down through Ludgate did he ride,
To catch the man who sold this dreadful Mutton.

Now to Fleet Market full of wrath he came;
And, with the spirit of an ancient Roman,
Exceeded I believe by no man,
The Alderman so virtuous cried out 'Shame!'

'Damme,' to Robinson said Master Skinner,
'Who on such Mutton, Sir, can make a dinner?' –
'*You*, if you please,'
Cried Mister Robinson with perfect ease.

'Sir!' quoth the red-hot Alderman again.
'*You*,' quoth the Hind, in just the same cool strain.

'Off, off,' cried Skinner, 'with your Carrion heap!
Quick, damme, take away your nasty Sheep.
While I command, not e'en the King
Shall such vile stuff to market bring,
And London stalls such garbage put on;
So please to take away your stinking Mutton.' –

'*You*,' replied Robinson, '*you* cry out Shame?
You blast the Sheep, good Master Skinner, pray?
You give the harmless Mutton a bad name?
You impudently order it away?

'*Sweet* Master Alderman, don't make this rout:
Pray clap your spectacles upon your snout;
And then your keen surveying eyes regale
With those same fine large letters on the cart
Which brought this *blasted* Mutton here for sale.' –
Poor Skinner read, and read it with a start.

Like Hamlet frighten'd at his Father's Ghost,
The Alderman stood staring like a Post:
He saw G.R. inscribed, in handsome letters,
Which proved the Sheep belong'd unto his *betters*.

The Alderman now turn'd to deep reflection;
And, being blest with *proper* recollection,
Exclaim'd: 'I've made a great *mistake*; oh! sad:
The Sheep are really not so *bad*.

'Dear Mister Robinson, I beg your pardon,
Your Job-like patience I've borne hard on:
Whoever says the Mutton is not good,
Knows nothing, Mister Robinson, of food.

'I verily believe I could turn glutton,
On such neat, wholesome, pretty-looking Mutton.
Pray, Mister Robinson, the Mutton sell.
I hope, Sir, that his Majesty is well.'

So saying, Mister Robinson he quitted,
With Cherubimic Smiles and placid brows,
For such embarrassing occasions fitted;
Adding just five and twenty humble Bows.

To work went Robinson to sell the Sheep;
But people would not buy, except dog-cheap:[32]

---

32 Indeed the mutton could only be sold for dog-meat.

At length the Sheep were sold, without the fleece;
And brought King George just Half-a-crown apiece.

Now for the other saucy *lying* Story;
Made, one would think, to tarnish Kingly glory.

The King and Parson Young

THE KING (God bless him) met old Parson Young
Walking on Windsor Terrace one fair morning:
Delightful was the day, the scent was strong;
A heavenly day for howling and for horning;
For tearing Farmers' hedges down, hallooings,
Shouts, curses, oaths, and such-like *pious* doings.

'Young,' cried the King, 'd'ye hunt, d'ye hunt to-day?
Yes, yes: what, what? yes, yes: fine day, fine day.'

Low with a reverent bow the Priest replied,
'Great King, I really have no Horse to ride:
Nothing, O Monarch, but my founder'd Mare;
And she, my Liege, as blind as she can stare.' –

'No horse?' rejoin'd the King: 'no horse, no horse?' –
'Indeed,' the Parson added, 'I have none:
Nothing but poor old Dobbin; who of course
Is dangerous, being blinder than a Stone.' –

'Blind, blind, Young? never mind: you must, must go;
Must hunt, must hunt, Young. Stay behind? no, no.' –
What pity that the King, in his discourse,
Forgot to say, 'I'll lend you, Young, a horse!'

The King to Young behaving thus so *kind*,
Whate'er the danger, and howe'er inclin'd,
At home with *politesse* Young could not stay:
So up his Reverence got upon the mare;
Resolv'd the chase with Majesty to share,
And risk the dangers of the day.

Roused was the Deer. The King and Parson Young,
Castor and Pollux like, rode side by side;
When, lo! a ditch was to be sprung:
Over leap'd George the Third with *kingly* pride.

Over leap'd Tinker, Tower, Rockwood, Towler,
Over leap'd Mend-all, Brushwood, Jubal, Jowler,
Trimbush and Lightning, Music, Ranter, Wonder,
And fifty others with their mouths of thunder;
Great names, whose Pedigrees so fair
With those of Homer's Heroes might compare.

Thus *gloriously* attended, leap'd the King;
By all those Hounds attended with a spring:
Not Cesar's self a fiercer look put on,
When with his Host he pass'd the Rubicon.

But wayward Fate the Parson's palfry humbled,
And gave the Mare a sudden check;
Unfortunately, poor blind Dobbin stumbled,
And broke his Reverence's neck.

The Monarch, gaping, with amaze look'd round
Upon his dead Companion on the ground.
'What, what?' he cried, 'Young dead? Young dead, Young *dead*?
Humph! take him up, and put him home to *bed*.'

Thus having finish'd, with a cheerful face
Nimrod the Second joined the jovial chase.

A MORAL REFLECTION

Fools would have *stopp'd* when Parson Young was kill'd,
And given up every thought of Hound and Deer;
And with a *weakness,* call'd Compassion, fill'd
Had turn'd *Samaritan,* and dropp'd a tear.

But *better* far the Royal Sportsman knew:
He guess'd the consequence, beyond a doubt;
Full well he guess'd he should not have a *view,*
And that he should be shamefully *thrown out.*

Perhaps from the Royal eye a tear *might* hop;
Yet Pages swear they never *saw* it drop.

But Majesty may say: 'What, what, what's death?
Nought, nought, nought but a little loss of breath.'

To Parson Young 'was *more*, I'm very clear:
He lost by death some hundred pounds a year.

from *The Royal Tour, and Weymouth Amusements. 1795*

A solemn and reprimanding Epistle to the Laureat
Aude/ Caesaris invicti dicere.[33] Horace

Shame on thee, Pye! To Caesar tune the string;
Berhyme his *route,* and Weymouth Wonders sing.
Saddle thy Pegasus at once, ride post:
Lo, ere thou start'st, a thousand things are *lost.*

The Royal Tour

SEE! Cesar's *off:* the dust around him hovers;
And gathering, lo, the King of Glory covers!
The Royal hubbub fills both eye and ear,
And wide-mouth'd Wonder marks the wild career. –
How like his golden *brother* of the Sky,
When Nature thunders, and the storm is high;
Now in, now out of clouds, behind, before,
Who rolls amid the elemental roar!

Heavens! with what ardour through the lanes he drives,
The country trembling for its tenants' lives!
Squat on his speckled haunches gapes the Toad,
And Frogs affrighted hop along the road:
The Hares astonish'd to their terrors yield,
Cock their long ears, and scud from field to field:
The Owl, loud hooting, from his ivy rushes;
And Sparrows, chattering, flutter from the bushes:

33 ['Dare to celebrate the achievements of invincible Caesar'.]

Old Women (call'd 'a pack of blinking bitches'),
Dash'd by the thundering Light-horse into ditches,
Scrambling and howling, with posteriors pointed
(Sad picture!) plump against the Lord's Anointed.
Dogs bark, Pigs grunt, the flying Turkeys gobble;
Fowls cackle; screaming Geese, with stretch'd wing, hobble;
Dire death his horses' hoofs to Ducklings deal,
And Goslings gasp beneath the burning wheel. –
Thus the great Eol, when he rushes forth,
With all his winds, east, west, and south, and north:
Flutter the leaves of trees, with woful fright,
Shook by his rage, and bullied by his might;
Straws from the lanes dispers'd, and whirl'd in air,
The blustering wonders of his mouth declare:
Heaved from their deep foundations, with dread sound
Barns and old houses thunder to the ground;
And bowing oaks, in ages rooted strong,
Roar through their branches as he sweeps along.
George breakfasts on the road, gulps tea, bolts toast;
Jokes with the Waiter, witty with the Host;
Runs to the Garden with his morning *dues*;
Makes mouths at Cloacina's;[34] reads the news.
Now mad for fruit, he scours the garden round;
Knocks every apple that he spies, to ground;
Loads every Royal pocket; seeks his chaise;
Plumps in, and fills the village with amaze.
He's *off* again: he smokes along the road.
Pursue him, Pye; pursue him with an *ode*:
And yet a *pastoral* might better please,
That talks of sheep and hay, and beans and peas;
Of trees cut down that Richmond's lawn adorn,
To gain the pittance of a peck of corn.[35]
He reaches Weymouth; treads the Esplanade:
Hark, hark, the jingling bells! the cannonade!
Drums beat, the hurdygurdies grind the air;
Dogs, cats, old women, all upon the stare.
All Weymouth gapes with wonder: hark, huzzas,
The roaring welcome of a thousand jaws!

---

34 [Cloacina: the Goddess of the lavatory and all lavatorial functions.]
35 Great has been the massacre among the *sturdy oaks*, to make room for the courtier-like *pliability* of the *corn-stalk*, that brings more *grist* to the Royal mill.

O Pye, shalt *thou*, Apollo's favourite son,
In loyalty by Peter be outdone?
How oft I bear thy Master on my back,
Without one thimbleful of cheering Sack;
While *thou* (not drunk, I hope), O Bard divine,
Oft wett'st thy whistle with the Muse's Wine!
Oh haste where prostrate Courtiers Monarchs greet,
Like Cats that seek the *sunshine* of the street;
Where Chesterfield, the lively Spaniel, springs,
Runs, leaps, and makes rare merriment for Kings;
Where sharp Macmanus, and sly Jealous, tread,
To guard from Treachery's blow the Royal head;[36]

Where Nunn and Barber,[37] silent as the Mouse,
Steal nightly *certain* goods to Gloucester House.
Oh say, shall Cesar in rare *presents* thrive,
Buy cheaper too than any man alive,
Go *cheaper* in excursions on the water,
And Laureat Pye know nothing of the matter?
Acts that should bid his Poet's bosom flame,
And make his *spendthrift* Subjects blush with shame!
What though Tom Warton laugh'd at Kings and Queens,
And grinning eyed them just as *state machines*;
Much better pleased (so sick of Royal life)
To celebrate Squire Punch, and Punch's Wife?
I grant thee deep in Attic, Latian lore;
Yet learn the province of the Muse of yore:
The Bards of ancient times (so History sings)
Eat, drank, and danced, and slept, with mighty Kings;
Who courted, reverenced, loved the tuneful throng,
And deem'd their deeds *ennobled* by a Song.

---

36 Be it recollected with horror, that a stone was flung at our beloved Sovereign in St James's Park, about two or three years past, endangering his life; yet an impudent Rhymer thought *otherwise*; who, on the occasion, had the audacity to write the following Epigram:

> Talk no more of the lucky escape of the *head*,
> From a flint so unwittingly thrown:
> I think very different, with thousands indeed;
> 'Twas a lucky escape for the *stone*.

37 Two Tradesmen who repair constantly from London to Weymouth, when Royalty deigns to visit the spot.

Lo, Pitt arrives: alas, with lantern face! –
'What, hæ, Pitt, hæ? what, Pitt hæ, *more* disgrace?' –
Ah, Sire, bad news! a second dire defeat:
Vendee undone, and all the Chouans beat.' –
'Hæ, hæ? what, what? beat, beat? what, beat agen?
Well, well, more money: raise more men, more men.
But mind, Pitt, hæ: mind, huddle up the news;
Coin something, and the growling Land amuse:
Make all the *sans-culottes* to Paris caper,
And Rose shall print the victory in his Paper.
Let's hear no more, no more of *Cornish* tales;
I sha'n't *refund* a guinea, Pitt, to Wales.
I can't afford it, no, I can't afford:
Wales cost a deal in pocket-cash and board.

'Pitt, Pitt, there's Frost, my bailiff Frost; see, see!
Well, Pitt, go back, go back again; b'ye, b'ye.
Keep London still, no matter how they carp:
Well, well, go back, and bid Dundas look sharp.
Must not lose France; no, France *must* wear a Crown:
If France won't swallow, *ram* a Monarch *down*.
Some *crowns* are scarce worth *sixpences*: hæ, Pitt?' –
The Premier smiled, and left the Royal wit.

Now Frost approaches: 'Well, Frost, well, Frost, pray,
How, how went sheep a score? how corn and hay?'

'An't please your Majesty, a *charming* price:
Corn very soon will be as dear as *spice*.'

'Thank God! but, say, say, do the Poor complain?
Hæ, hæ, will wheat be *sixpence*, Frost, *a grain*?'

'I hope *not*, Sire; for great were then my fears,
That Windsor would be pull'd about our ears.'

'Frost, Frost, no politics; no, no, Frost, no:
You, you talk politics! oho, oho!
Windsor come down about our ears! what, what?
D'ye think, hæ, hæ, that I'm afraid of that?
What, what are Soldiers good for, but *obey*?
Macmanus, Townsend, Jealous, hæ, hæ, hæ?

Pull Windsor down? hæ, what? a pretty job!
Windsor be pull'd to pieces by the Mob!
Talk, talk of farming; that's your *forte,* d'ye see:
And, mind, mind, *politics* belong to *me.*
Go back, go back, and watch the Windsor chaps;
Count all the poultry: set, set well the *traps.*

'See, see, see Stacie![38] Here, here, Stacie, here:
Going to market, Stacie? dear, dear, dear!
I get all *my* provision by the *mail.*[39]
Hæ, money plenty, Stacie? don't fear jail.
Rooms, rooms all full? hæ, hæ, no beds to spare?
What, what! give travellers, hæ, good fare, good fare?
Good sign, good sign, to have no empty beds:
Shows, shows that people like to see Crown'd Heads'.

The Mail arrives: hark, hark, the cheerful horn,
To Majesty announcing oil and corn,
Turnips and cabbages, and soap and candles;
And, lo, each article great Cesar handles!
Bread, cheese, salt, ketchup, vinegar, and mustard,
Small beer and bacon, apple-pie and custard:
All, all, from Windsor greets his *frugal* Grace,
For Weymouth is a damn'd *expensive* place.
Salisbury appears, the lord of stars and strings;
Presents his Poem to the Best of Kings.[40]
Great Cesar reads it; feels a *laughing* fit,
And wonders Salisbury should become a *wit.*

A batch of Bullocks! See great Cesar run:
He stops the Drover; *bargain* is begun.
He feels their ribs and rumps; he shakes his head:
'Poor, Drover, poor; poor, very poor, indeed.'

38 The honest master of the Royal Hotel.
39 This Mail-coach costs the Public at least *fifty pounds* every *day* of the week
   (Sundays not excepted) during the King's residence at Weymouth. It is really a
   sutler's cart.
40 This *high* Lord is really a *high* Poet. His 'Journey to Weymouth,' which I was
   horribly afraid would have *forestalled* mine with the Public, will makes its
   appearance soon; and, I am informed, will be enriched, *like my works* (O marvel-
   ling Reader! most elegantly bound at this time, and in the Library at
   Buckingham-House) with *royal annotation.*

Cesar and Drover haggle; difference split:
How much? a shilling: what a *royal* hit!

A load of Hay in sight: great Cesar flies;
Smells, shakes his head: '*Bad* hay, *sour* hay.' He *buys*.
'Smell, Courtown, smell; *good bargain, lucky* load:
Smell Courtown; *sweeter* hay was never mow'd.'

A herd of Swine goes by. 'Whose hogs are these?
Hæ, farmer, hæ?' – 'Yours, measter, if yow pleaze.' –
'*Poor*, farmer, poor; *lean, lousy*, very poor:
Sell, sell, hæ, sell?' – 'Iss, measter, to be zure:
My pigs were made for zale, but what o' that?
Yow caall mun *lean*: now, zur, I caall mun *vat*.
Measter, I baant a starling, can't be cort;
You think, agosh, to ha the pigs vor *nort*.' –
Lo! Cesar *buys* the pigs; he slily winks:
'Hæ, Gwynne, the fellow is not *caught*, he thinks.
Fool, not to know the *bargain* I have got!
Hæ, Gwynne, nice bargain? lucky, lucky lot!'

Enter the Dancing Dogs: they take their stations;
They bow, they curtsey, to the Lord of Nations;
They dance, they skip, they charm the King of Fun,
While Courtiers see themselves almost *outdone*.

Lord Paulet enters on his hands and knees,
Joining the *hunts* of *hares* with *hunts* of *fleas*.[41]

Enter Sir Joseph, gladdening Royal eyes:
What holds his hand? a box of Butterflies,
Grubs, nests and eggs of humming-birds, to please;
Newts, tadpoles, brains of beetles, stings of bees:
The noble President without a bib on,
To sport the glories of his *blushing* Ribbon.

The Fishermen, the Fishermen behold!
A shoal of fish: the men their nets unfold;

41 The Earl has won the *royal smile*, and is made Lord of the Bedchamber; but, as
capricious inconstancy is a prominent feature in the Brunswick family, a *royal
frown* may be at no great distance.

Surround the scaly fry; they drag to land:
Cesar and Co. rush down upon the sand.
The fishes leap about: Gods, what a clatter!
Cesar, delighted, jumps into the water:
He *marvels* at the fish with *fins* and *scales*;
He plunges at them, seizes heads and tails;
Enjoys the draught: he capers, laughs aloud,
And shows his captives to the gaping crowd.
He orders them to Gloucester Lodge; they go:
But are the Fishermen rewarded? – *No.*

Cesar spies Lady Cathcart with a book:
He flies to know what 'tis; he longs to look.
'What's in your hand, my Lady? let me know.' –
'A book, an't please your Majesty.' – 'Oho!
Book's a good thing, good thing. I like a book.
Very good thing, my Lady: let me look.
War of America, my Lady, hæ?
Bad thing, my Lady: fling, fling *that* away.'

A Sailor pops upon the Royal Pair,
On crutches borne, an object of despair:
His squalid beard, pale cheek, and haggard eye,
Though silent, pour for *help* a piercing cry.
'Who, who are *you*? what, what? hæ, what are you?' –
'A *man*, my Liege, whom kindness never knew.' –
'A sailor, sailor, hæ? you've lost a leg.' –
'I know it, Sire; which forces me to beg.
I've nine poor children, Sir, besides a wife;
God bless them! the sole comforts of my life.' –

'Wife and nine children, hæ? all, all alive?
No, no, no wonder that you cannot thrive.
Shame, shame, to fill your hut with such a train!
Shame to get brats for *others* to maintain![42]
Get, get a wooden leg, or one of cork:
Wood's *cheapest*; yes, get wood, and go to work.
But mind, mind, Sailor; hæ, hæ, hæ? hear, hear:
Don't go to Windsor, mind, and *cut* one there:

---

42 Is not this sarcasm as applicable to *thrones* as to *hovels*?

That's dangerous, dangerous; there I place my *traps*;
Fine things, fine things, for legs of *thieving* chaps.
Best traps, *my* traps: take care; they *bite*, they bite,
And sometimes catch a *dozen legs* a night.' –
'Oh had I money, Sir, to *buy* a leg!' –
'No money, hæ? *nor I*. Go beg, go beg.'
How sweetly *kind*, to bid the Cripple *mump*,
And cut from *other people's* trees a stump!
[...]
'Mine Gote, your Mashesty! Don't hear sush stuff:
De Workhouse always geefs de Poor *enough*.
Why make bout dirty leg sush wondrous fuss?
And den, what *impudence* for beg of *us!*
In Strelitz, O mine Gote! de Beggar skip:
Dere, for a *sharity*, we geefs a *whip*.
Money make Subshects impudent, I'm sure:
Respect be always where de Peepel's *poor*.'

'How, Sailor, did you lose your leg? hæ, hæ?'
'I lost it, please your Majesty, at sea,
Hard fighting for my Country and my King.'
'Hæ, what? That's *common*, very common thing.
Hæ! *lucky* fellow, that you were not *drill'd:*
Some lose their heads, and many men are kill'd.
Your parish? Where's your parish? hæ? where, where?' –
'I served my prenticeship in Manchester.' –
'Fine town, fine town; full, full of trade and riches:
Hæ, sailor, hæ, can you make leather breeches?
These come from Manchester: there, there I got 'em.'
(On which great Cesar smacks his buckskin bottom.)
'Must not *encourage* vagrants; no, no, no:
Must not make laws, my lad, and break 'em too.
Where, where's your parish, hæ? And where's your pass?
Well, make haste home: I've got, I've got no brass.'

Now to the Esplanade a seat is borne,
To ease the Queen's sweet bottom and her corn;
For corns are apt even *majesty* to bite,
As well as on *poor* toes to vent their spite.
[...]
The Stadholder! He joins Queen Charlotte: *bump*
Falls on the seat of Royalty his rump.

Peace to his spirit! he begins to doze:
He snores; Heavens bless the Trumpet of his Nose!
So great is folly, that the World mayhap
Shall grinning point at Hoogen Moogen's *nap*.
Princes of Europe, pray exclaim not 'Shame!'
Go, for Mankind's repose, and *do the same*.
[…]
Hark! Cesar and the little Children talk;
Together laugh, together too they walk:
The Mob around admire their pleasant things,
And *marle* that *children* talk as *well* as *kings*.

And now to Delamot's the Monarch speeds:
He catches up a score of books, and reads;
Learns *nothing*; sudden quits the book-abode,
Orders his horse, and scours the Dorset road.
He's in again: he boards the barge; sets sail;
Jokes with the Sailors, and enjoys the gale:
Descants on winds and waves, the land regains,
And gives the Tars – just *nothing*, for their pains;
For what a *bore* that Kings their *slaves* should *pay*!
Sufficient is the *honour* of the day.
Now springs the Sovereign wildly to the seas;
Rushes intrepid in, *along to knees*.
Old Neptune, jealous of his world, looks big;
And blustering Boreas blows away his wig.

*

O PYE! amidst such doings canst thou *sleep*?
Such Wonders *whelping* on the land and deep;
So nobly form'd to deck th' historic page,
Astonish Man, and swell the Muse's rage!
Thus, thus *I* sing of Royalty, *unpaid*;
In Courts observe, and follow to the shade:
And mean, God willing, since *thou* wilt not write,
To give each word and action to the light;
With daily deeds my voice sublimely raise,
And sound *wise speeches* into distant days.
In spite of low Democracy, the brute,
Kings shall at length regain their *lost* repute.

Fyfield*Books*

Two millennia of essential classics
The extensive Fyfield*Books* list includes

Djuna Barnes *The Book of Repulsive Women and other poems*
edited by Rebecca Loncraine

Elizabeth Barrett Browning *Selected Poems* edited by Malcolm Hicks

Charles Baudelaire *Complete Poems in French and English*
translated by Walter Martin

The Brontë Sisters *Selected Poems* edited by Stevie Davies

Lewis Carroll *Selected Poems* edited by Keith Silver

Thomas Chatterton *Selected Poems* edited by Grevel Lindop

John Clare *By Himself* edited by Eric Robinson and David Powell

Samuel Taylor Coleridge *Selected Poetry* edited by William Empson and David Pirie

John Donne *Selected Letters* edited by P.M. Oliver

Oliver Goldsmith *Selected Writings* edited by John Lucas

Victor Hugo *Selected Poetry in French and English*
translated by Steven Monte

Wyndham Lewis *Collected Poems and Plays* edited by Alan Munton

Charles Lamb *Selected Writings* edited by J.E. Morpurgo

Ben Jonson *Epigrams and The Forest* edited by Richard Dutton

Giacomo Leopardi *The Canti with a selection of his prose*
translated by J.G. Nichols

Andrew Marvell *Selected Poems* edited by Bill Hutchings

Charlotte Mew *Collected Poems and Selected Prose*
edited by Val Warner

Michelangelo *Sonnets* translated by Elizabeth Jennings, introduction by Michael Ayrton

William Morris *Selected Poems* edited by Peter Faulkner

Ovid *Amores* translated by Tom Bishop

Edgar Allan Poe *Poems and Essays on Poetry*
edited by C.H. Sisson

Restoration Bawdy edited by John Adlard

Rainer Maria Rilke *Sonnets to Orpheus and Letters to a Young Poet*
translated by Stephen Cohn

Christina Rossetti *Selected Poems* edited by C.H. Sisson

Sir Walter Scott *Selected Poems* edited by James Reed

Sir Philip Sidney *Selected Writings* edited by Richard Dutton

Henry Howard, Earl of Surrey *Selected Poems*
edited by Dennis Keene

Algernon Charles Swinburne *Selected Poems*
edited by L.M. Findlay

Oscar Wilde *Selected Poems* edited by Malcolm Hicks

Sir Thomas Wyatt *Selected Poems* edited by Hardiman Scott

For more information, including a full list of Fyfield*Books* and a contents list for each title, and details of how to order the books, visit the Carcanet website at www.carcanet.co.uk or email info@carcanet.co.uk